GERMAN REVISION FOR JUNIOR CERTIFICATE
(Higher Level)

BERNADETTE MATTHEWS AND MADELEINE O'NEILL

GILL & MACMILLAN

Gill & Macmillan Ltd
Hume Avenue
Park West
Dublin 12
with associated companies throughout the world
www.gillmacmillan.ie

© Bernadette Matthews and Madeleine O'Neill 2005
Illustrations pp. 15, 27, 34, 66, 109 and 115 © Kate Shannon

0 7171 3835 6
Print origination in Ireland by
Carrigboy Typesetting Services, Co. Cork

*The paper used in this book is made from the wood pulp of managed forests. For every
tree felled, at least one tree is planted, thereby renewing natural resources.*

ACKNOWLEDGMENTS

The authors and publisher are grateful to the following for
permission to reproduce copyright material:

Extract from *Als Hitler das rosa Kaninchen stahl* by Judith Kerr published by HarperCollins
Publishers Ltd. Reprinted by permission of HarperCollins Publishers Ltd.
© 1971 Judith Kerr; 'Verlorene Kindheit' aus ZEITLUPE Nr.: 34 „Eine Welt"
Hrsg.: Bundeszentrale für politische Bildung/bpb, Bonn.

PHOTO CREDITS

For permission to reproduce photographs and other material,
the author and publisher gratefully acknowledge the following:

42, 99, 111, 120, 147 © Alamy Images; 89 © Bubbles/Frans Rombout; Corbis: 38 © Adam
Woolfitt, 106 © Felix Zaska; v, 1, 45 © educationphotos.co.uk; 6, 10, 20, 80, 124, 139, 155
© Imagefile Ireland; 127 © Inpho; 125 © Lonely Planet Images/Diana Mayfield; 31
© Reuters/Ina Fassbender; 22 © Travelsite/Neil Setchfield

The author and publisher have made every effort to trace all copyright holders,
but if any has been inadvertently overlooked we would be pleased to
make the necessary arrangements at the first opportunity.

CONTENTS

Introduction   v
Exam Layout   vi

1. Listening Comprehension (Aural)   1
Exam tips   2
List of Topics   3
Vocabulary Under Topic Headings   3

2. Reading Comprehension   45
Exam Tips   46
Section A   47
Section B   50
Section C   58
Section D   66
Section E   72
Section F   76
Section G   83
Solutions to 'Test Yourself' Questions   93
Solutions to Past Exam Questions   96

3. Written Expression   99
Exam Tips   100
A (Letter)   101
B (Shorter Exercise)   139

4. Examination Papers   156

INTRODUCTION

The Junior Certificate Examination is the first big exam you will sit and for many young people it is a daunting prospect. This revision book aims to help you feel confident in facing the Higher Level German paper.

The book is divided into four sections. The first three sections deal with the areas examined in the Junior Certificate, i.e. Listening Comprehension (Aural), Reading Comprehension and Written Expression. There are guidelines about timing, suggestions about relevant vocabulary and other useful tips. Each section includes an indication of how the marks are allocated. The fourth section contains a complete exam paper with solutions and marks. An additional recent exam paper is also provided.

VIEL SPASS BEIM LERNEN!

EXAM LAYOUT

The Junior Certificate Higher Level German exam lasts two and a half hours and has three sections. *All questions must be answered*, so you will lose no time in deciding which ones to do!

	Marks	Per Cent
1. Listening Comprehension (Aural)	140	44 (approx.)
2. Reading Comprehension	100	31 (approx.)
3. Written Expression	80	25
Total	*320*	*100*

1. Listening Comprehension

The Listening Comprehension test is the first part of the German exam which takes place in June. It tests your ability to understand spoken German. The Listening test lasts approximately 30–40 minutes and when it is finished, you proceed immediately to sections 2 and 3. *Questions are asked and answered in English.*

2. Reading Comprehension

This part of the exam tests your ability to understand different types of written German. There are seven sections, A–G, which increase in volume and level of difficulty. The earlier sections include notices, advertisements and school language, while the later ones have longer passages of German text. *Questions are asked and answered in English.*

3. Written Expression

This is the only section of the exam where you must produce some actual German yourself. Here you are asked to write a letter and a short note or postcard.

1. LISTENING COMPREHENSION (AURAL)

(140 marks)

This section of the book aims to help you to be fully prepared for the Listening test. It presents in a clear and simple format the topics and relevant vocabulary generally examined at Junior Certificate Higher Level German. Each topic is given a separate heading, for example SCHOOL, SHOPPING, TIME. Of course, some words may apply to several topics and in such cases appear only once here. If you revise thoroughly the vocabulary under each heading and learn anything that is new to you, you will be able to approach the Listening test with confidence. Transcripts of some dialogues from recent exams are included here to let you see how true this is.

As the task is to understand what you hear, there is less emphasis in this part of the book on words which may sound the same in English, such as 'Hotel', 'Disco' or 'Taxi'.

Of course, the vocabulary included in this section will be invaluable to you in all parts of the exam. For this reason, the *German* definite articles 'der', 'die' and 'das' are given to indicate gender of nouns. You will also find a great number of adjectives throughout the various topics covered.

If you use some of those in the Written Expression test, your writing will be greatly enriched.

Obviously, the best way to improve your understanding of spoken German is to hear lots of it. If you have no contact with native German speakers, you should use every opportunity to listen to German on tape, CD, radio, television or film.

Exam Tips

1. The tape starts with a short introduction, giving the name and year of your exam. If, for any reason, you cannot hear this introduction clearly, you should tell the supervisor, as you are not allowed to make any comment or to interrupt while the tape is playing. There is rarely a problem.

2. Concentration is essential here. You have no time for looking around to see how others are doing. Instead you must focus your attention on the questions asked on the paper and on what you are hearing on the tape.

3. You will have enough time to prepare for each section of the test, but you must use that time wisely. Of course, you are tired of being told to read the questions carefully. However, your reading will involve an element of planning for what you are about to hear. For example, if the question asks 'when' something will happen, you know to expect to hear an expression of time, such as the time of day or week or season, etc. and you can feel confident that you will recognise the relevant vocabulary. It is useful to underline a question word such as 'When?' so that you do not answer 'Where?' by mistake!

4. Reading the paper includes paying careful attention to the instructions given at the start of each of the five sections A–E. They will clearly indicate how many times the section will be played, i.e. *twice* or *three times*. When the piece is played three times, the second playing has built-in pauses, giving you time to write your answers. Pieces played twice only are shorter and less demanding and you will have plenty of time to fill in the answers.

5. As the questions on the paper are in English, your answers should also be in English. This is very important, because if you answer in German, you lose marks, even though the information may be correct.

6. You rarely have to write a full sentence in answering the Listening test. In fact, some answers may require just a word or a short phrase. However, where you are asked to 'give details', it is obvious that a fuller answer is needed.

7. Be clear in the presentation of your answers. Your writing should be legible and your answers should leave no doubt in the mind of the examiner as to what you intended. Be sure to put each answer in the correct space provided.

VIEL GLÜCK!

List of Topics

- Personal Details
- Family and Pets
- Home
- Hobbies/Leisure
- School
- Careers/Jobs
- Penpals and Exchanges
- Transport
- In Town
- Numbers
- Time
- Seeking Accommodation
- Weather
- Illness and Accidents
- Clothes
- Shopping
- Food and Drink

Vocabulary Under Topic Headings

PERSONAL DETAILS

Name

Ich heiße . . .
Ich bin Martin/Martina.

(veirstehn)
februar .

Age

Ich bin vierzehn Jahre alt.
Ich bin fünfzehn.
Ich werde bald sechzehn sein.   I will soon be sixteen.

Place in Family

Ich bin der/die jüngste } in der Familie.
      älteste

Birthday

Ich habe am ersten Mai
    dritten Juni } Geburtstag.
    zwanzigsten März

Appearance

Adjectives used to describe *hair:*

lang	long	schwarz	black	grau	grey
kurz	short	braun	brown	hellbraun	light brown
lockig	curly	rot	red	dunkelblond	dark blond
glatt	straight	blond	blond		

Ich habe lange braune Haare.
Ich habe kurze blonde Haare.

Adjectives used to describe *eyes*:

blau	blue
grün	green
braun	brown
grau	grey

Ich habe grüne Augen.
Ich trage eine Brille.   I wear glasses.

Adjectives used to describe *size*:

groß	tall	**dick**	fat
klein	small	**dünn**	thin
mittelgroß	of medium height	**schlank**	slim

Ich bin groß. Ich bin ein Meter siebzig.

Other adjectives used to describe *appearance*:

schön	beautiful
hübsch	pretty
gut aussehend	good-looking

Personality

Adjectives used here include:

egoistisch	selfish	**lustig**	funny
ehrlich	honest	**neidisch**	envious
eifersüchtig	jealous	**nett/sympathisch**	nice
freundlich	friendly	**schüchtern**	shy
glücklich	happy	**treu**	loyal
launisch	moody	**witzig**	witty/funny

FAMILY AND PETS

Parents and Siblings

die Mutter + der Vater = die Eltern
eine Schwester, ein Bruder = die Geschwister
Ich habe eine Schwester und einen Bruder.
Ich bin Einzelkind.   I am an only child.
Ich habe keine Geschwister.   I have no brothers and sisters.

If you hear the prefix 'Zwilling', it means 'twin' as in 'Ich habe einen Zwillingsbruder'.

Meine Eltern sind geschieden.	My parents are divorced.
Ich wohne bei meiner Mutter/ meinem Vater.	I live with my mother/my father.
Mein Bruder ist verheiratet.	My brother is married.

Other Family Members

Masculine		Feminine	
dér Sohn	son	**die Tochter**	daughter
der Onkel	uncle	**die Tante**	aunt
der Vetter/Cousin	cousin	**die Cousine**	cousin
der Neffe	nephew	**die Nichte**	niece
der Großvater (Opa)	grandfather	**die Großmutter (Oma)**	grandmother
der Enkelsohn	grandson	**die Enkeltochter**	granddaughter

Plural	
die Kinder	children
die Enkelkinder	grandchildren
die Großeltern	grandparents
die Verwandten	relatives

Pets

Ich habe/Wir haben:

einen Hund	a dog	**einen Wellensittich**	a budgie
eine weiße Maus	a white mouse	**einen Goldfisch**	a goldfish
einen Papagei	a parrot	**ein Meerschweinchen**	a guinea pig
eine Katze	a cat	**einen Hamster**	a hamster
ein Kaninchen	a rabbit	**eine Schildkröte**	a turtle
einen Kanarienvogel	a canary		

Wir haben kein Haustier.	We have no pet.
Mein Bruder hat Angst vor Hunden.	My brother is afraid of dogs.
Unsere Katze ist gestorben.	Our cat has died.
Mein Papagei ist tot.	My parrot is dead.

Ich komme aus Irland.

Ich wohne in Irland.

Farm Animals

die Kuh	cow	**das Pferd**	horse
das Schaf	sheep	**das Huhn**	hen
das Schwein	pig	**der Esel**	donkey

HOME

Country, State, City, Town

Deutschland	Germany
Ich komme aus Deutschland.	I come from Germany.
Österreich	Austria
Ich wohne in Österreich.	I live in Austria.
die Schweiz	Switzerland
Ich wohne in/komme aus der Schweiz.	I live in/come from Switzerland.

Apart from these countries where German is spoken, the names of states, cities or towns may be heard in the Listening test, e.g.

States: **Bayern**   Bavaria

Cities: **Wien**   Vienna
            München   Munich

Towns: **Emden**
            Passau

For a list of other countries, please refer to section on PENPALS AND EXCHANGES (p. 19).

Location

Ich wohne/Wir wohnen:	
in der Stadt	in town
in der Stadtmitte	in the town centre
in der Nähe von	near
nicht weit von	not far from
nicht weit von der Grenze	not far from the border
in der Hauptstraße	in the main street
in einem Dorf	in a village
auf dem Land	in the country
auf einem Bauernhof	on a farm
fünf Kilometer von Stuttgart entfernt	five kilometres from Stuttgart
zehn Gehminuten von der Stadtmitte	ten minutes' walk from the town centre
außerhalb der Stadt	outside the town
am Stadtrand	on the outskirts of town

House/Apartment

das Haus	house	**das Doppelhaus**	semi-detached house
die Wohnung	apartment	**das Reihenhaus**	terraced house
der Wohnblock	apartment block	**im Erdgeschoss**	on the ground floor
das Einfamilienhaus	detached house	**im zweiten Stock**	on the second floor

Der gang - Corridor

Around the House

das Zimmer	room	**der Garten**	garden
die Küche	kitchen	**der Boden/Fußboden**	floor
das Schlafzimmer	bedroom	**die Treppe**	stairs
der Dachboden	attic	**die Tür**	door
das Wohnzimmer	living room	**das Fenster**	window
der Flur	hall	**die Vorhänge**	curtains
das Esszimmer	dining room	**die Mauer**	wall (outdoors)
der Keller	basement	**die Wand**	wall (indoors)
das Badezimmer	bathroom	**die Wände**	walls
das Dach	roof		

Furniture and Appliances

Im Schlafzimmer

das Bett	bed
die Bettdecke	blanket/quilt
das Kopfkissen	pillow
der Nachttisch	bedside table
der Schreibtisch	writing desk
der Kleiderschrank	wardrobe
der Wecker	alarm clock
die Lampe	lamp
das Bücherregal	bookshelf
der Frisiertisch	dressing table

Im Badezimmer

die Badewanne	bath
die Dusche	shower
die Toilette	toilet
das Waschbecken	washbasin
der Spiegel	mirror
das Handtuch	hand towel
das Badetuch	bath towel

Im Wohnzimmer

der Sessel	armchair
das Kissen	cushion
der Fernseher	television
der CD-Spieler	CD player
der Teppich	carpet

In der Küche

der Tisch	table
der Stuhl	chair
der Küchenschrank	kitchen cupboard
der Herd	cooker
der Backofen	oven

der Mikrowellenherd	microwave	das Geschirr	dishes
der Wäschetrockner	clothes drier	der Teller	plate
die Spülmaschine	dishwasher	die Tasse	cup
das Spülbecken	kitchen sink	die Untertasse	saucer
die Waschmaschine	washing machine	die Schüssel	bowl
der Kühlschrank	fridge		
die Tiefkühltruhe	freezer	das Besteck	cutlery
der Staubsauger	vacuum cleaner	das Messer	knife
das Bügeleisen	iron	die Gabel	fork
die Schublade	drawer	der Löffel	spoon

Household Chores

Ich räume mein Zimmer auf.	I tidy my room.
Meine Schwester putzt das Badezimmer.	My sister cleans the bathroom.
Mein Bruder saugt Staub.	My brother vacuums.
Meine Mutter arbeitet im Garten.	My mother works in the garden.
Sie mäht den Rasen.	She mows the lawn.
Mein Vater kocht.	My father cooks.
Ich bügele mein Hemd.	I iron my shirt.
Wir spülen ab./Wir waschen ab.	We wash up.
Ich decke den Tisch.	I set the table.
Sie räumt den Tisch ab.	She clears the table.
Wir füttern den Hund.	We feed the dog.
Er wäscht das Auto.	He washes the car.
Ich mache die Küche sauber.	I clean the kitchen.

Adjectives used here include:

bequem	comfortable	sauber	clean
ruhig	quiet	schmutzig	dirty
gemütlich	cosy	ordentlich	tidy
hell	bright		

HOBBIES/LEISURE

Ich lese.	I read.
Sie liest.	She reads.
Ich spiele Tennis.	I play tennis.
Er spielt Klavier.	He plays the piano.
Ich sehe fern.	I watch television.

Ich male.	I paint.
Ich zeichne.	I draw.
Ich schwimme.	I swim.
Ich segle.	I sail.
Ich fahre/laufe Schlittschuh.	I ice-skate.
Er fährt/läuft Rollschuh.	He roller-skates.
Ich fahre Rad.	I cycle.
Sie fährt Rad.	She cycles.
Ich sammle Münzen.	I collect coins.
Ich gehe ins Kino.	I go to the cinema.
Ich treibe/mache Sport.	I do sport.
Ich tanze.	I dance.
Ich gehe spazieren.	I go for a walk.
Wir machen einen Ausflug.	We go on a trip/outing.
Im Sommer fahren wir ans Meer.	In summer we go to the sea.

Other useful vocabulary for this topic:

Tischtennis	table tennis
Korbball/Basketball	basketball

Federball	badminton
die Geige	violin
die Flöte	flute
die Blockflöte	recorder
die Blechflöte	tin whistle
die Klarinette	clarinet
das Schlagzeug	drum
der Roman	novel
die Zeitung	newspaper
das Modejournal	fashion magazine
die Zeitschrift	magazine
die Serie	series
die Seifenoper	soap/serial
der Trickfilm	cartoon
der Spielfilm	feature film
der Dokumentarfilm	documentary
die Komödie	comedy
die Nachrichten	news
die Musiksendung	music programme
die Kindersendung	children's programme
das Wandern	hill-walking
das Reiten	horse riding
das Zelten	camping
die Umwelt	environment
der Urlaub	holiday
das Abenteuer	adventure

Likes and Dislikes

Ich mag	I like
Ich mag Sport.	
Ich mag Popmusik.	
Ich mag Krimis nicht.	I don't like crime stories.
Ich interessiere mich für	I am interested in
Ich interessiere mich für Filme.	
Ich finde Bergsteigen toll.	I think mountain climbing is great.
Ich hasse Rockmusik.	I hate rock music.
Ich kann Sportsendungen nicht leiden.	I can't stand sports programmes.

'Spaß machen' is used to say something is fun or enjoyable, e.g.

Das Lesen macht mir Spaß.   I enjoy reading.

Das Wandern macht uns Spaß.   We enjoy hill-walking.

Note: If the word 'gern' is used with a *verb*, it means that the person *likes* that activity. 'Nicht gern' expresses *dislike*, e.g.

Ich lese gern.	I like reading.
Er spielt gern Schach.	He likes playing chess.
Ich sehe gern fern.	I like watching television.
Sie läuft gern Ski.	She likes skiing.
Mein Vater angelt gern.	My father likes fishing.
In meiner Freizeit höre ich gern Musik.	I like listening to music in my free time.
Ich treibe nicht gern Sport.	I don't like doing sport.

Preferences and Favourites

If you hear 'lieber' with the verb, a *preference* is being expressed, e.g.

Ich spiele lieber Tennis.

Mein Bruder spielt lieber Fußball.

Ich höre lieber klassische Musik.

The expression 'am liebsten' may be heard. This indicates what the person likes doing *best*, e.g.

Ich spiele am liebsten Gitarre.

Sie liest am liebsten Zeitschriften.

Am liebsten spiele ich Volleyball.

Another way used in German to talk about a *favourite* is the prefix 'Lieblings-' followed by a noun:

Mein Lieblingssport ist Fußball.

Mein Lieblingsfilm ist ,,Herr der Ringe".

Meine Lieblingssendung ist ,,Wer wird Millionär?"

Meine Lieblingsgruppe ist U2.

Adjectives:

interessant	interesting		**neu**	new
spannend	exciting		**blöd/doof**	stupid
lustig	funny		**langweilig**	boring
alt	old		**traurig**	sad

SCHOOL

School Types

der Kindergarten	play school
die Grundschule	primary school
die Sekundarstufe:	second level
die Hauptschule	
die Realschule	
das Gymnasium	
die Gesamtschule	

School Life

Die Schule beginnt um acht Uhr.	School starts at eight o'clock.
Eine Stunde dauert fünfundvierzig Minuten.	A lesson lasts forty-five minutes. *vierzehn (40 min)*
Wir haben sechs Stunden am Tag.	We have six lessons a day.
Die Schule endet um ein Uhr. / Die Schule ist um ein Uhr aus.	School is over at one o'clock.
Wir haben den Nachmittag frei.	We are free in the afternoon.
Wir haben nur vormittags Schule.	We have school in the mornings only.
Wir tragen keine Uniform.	We don't wear a uniform.
Ich bin in der achten Klasse.	I am in the eighth year.

Other relevant vocabulary:

das Klassenzimmer	classroom
die Turnhalle	gym
das Labor	laboratory
das Sprachlabor	language laboratory
das Lehrerzimmer	staffroom
Schüler/in	pupil
Lehrer/in	teacher
Klassenlehrer/in	class teacher
Schulleiter/in, Schuldirektor/in	principal
der Stundenplan	timetable
die Pause	break

die Klassenarbeit/Arbeit	test
die Hausaufgaben	homework
der Unterricht	teaching/lessons
das Examen/die Prüfung	examination
das Schulhalbjahr	term
das Abitur	exam at end of 'Gymnasium'
das Zeugnis	report
die Klassenfahrt	class trip
die Tafel	blackboard
das Heft	copy
der Schreibblock	writing pad
der Kugelschreiber/Kuli	pen
der Bleistift	pencil
der Radiergummi	rubber
das Lineal	ruler
der Spitzer	pencil sharpener
das Notizbuch	notebook
der Taschenrechner	pocket calculator
der Filzstift	marker/felt pen
das Etui	pencil case
die Schultasche	schoolbag

Subjects

das Fach/die Fächer	subject/subjects
die Fremdsprachen	foreign languages
Deutsch	German
Französisch	French
Englisch	English
Spanisch	Spanish
Russisch	Russian
Latein	Latin
Naturwissenschaft	science
Biologie	biology
Chemie	chemistry
Physik	physics
Mathe(matik)	mathematics
Informatik	computer studies
Hauswirtschaft	home economics

Wirtschaftslehre	business studies
Geschichte	history
Erdkunde/Geographie	geography
Kunst	art
Religion	religion
Sport	P.E.

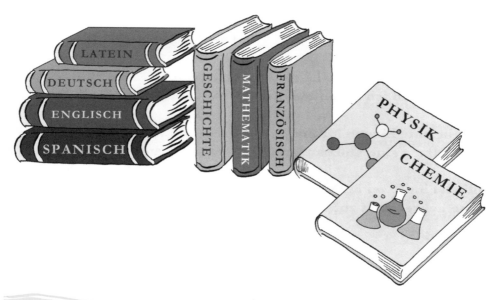

Mein Lieblingsfach ist Geschichte.	My favourite subject is history.
Meine Lieblingsfächer sind Kunst und Erdkunde.	My favourite subjects are art and geography.
Ich mag Fremdsprachen.	I like foreign languages.
Französisch gefällt mir.	I like French.
Ich kann Mathe nicht leiden.	I can't stand maths.
Informatik finde ich interessant.	I find computer studies interesting.
Grammatik finde ich schwer.	I find grammar hard.
Ich finde Wirtschaftslehre langweilig.	I find business studies boring.
Biologie ist nützlich.	Biology is useful.
Sport ist wichtig für die Gesundheit.	Sport is important for health.
Der Englischunterricht macht Spaß.	I enjoy English class./English class is fun.
Unser/e Deutschlehrer/in ist streng.	Our German teacher is strict.
Der Kunstlehrer ist immer guter Laune.	The art teacher is always in a good mood.

Marks and Reactions

The German marking system is very simple. Instead of percentages or A–F, a scale of 1–6 is used. 1 is the best mark and 6 the worst. This is how they are said: eine Eins, eine Zwei, eine Drei, eine Vier, eine Fünf, eine Sechs.

Ich habe eine Fünf in Englisch.	I've got a 5 in English.
Mein Vater ist wütend/enttäuscht.	My father is furious/disappointed.
Ich brauche Nachhilfe.	I need grinds.
Schon wieder eine Sechs!	Another 6!
Vielleicht muß ich sitzen bleiben.	I may have to repeat a year.
Ich habe eine Eins in Mathe.	I've got a 1 in maths.
Meine Eltern sind stolz auf mich.	My parents are proud of me.
Endlich eine Zwei in Deutsch!	At last a 2 in German!
Meine Lehrerin ist zufrieden.	My teacher is pleased.

Adjectives:

begabt	gifted/talented
anstrengend	demanding
richtig	right/correct
falsch	wrong/incorrect
nett	nice
lustig	funny
geduldig	patient
hilfsbereit	helpful
froh	happy
böse/ärgerlich	angry
verständnisvoll	understanding
ausgezeichnet	excellent
faul	lazy
fleißig	diligent, hard-working
schwierig	difficult
einfach/leicht	easy

CAREERS/JOBS

der Beruf	career/profession
die Stelle	job/position
Arzt/Ärztin	doctor
Tierarzt	veterinary surgeon
Zahnarzt	dentist
Bäcker/in	baker
Bankangestellter/Bankangestellte	bank official
Bauer	farmer
Landwirt/in	farmer
Briefträger/Postbote	postman
Briefträgerin/Postbotin	postwoman
Buchhalter/in	accountant
Busfahrer/in	bus driver
Friseur/Friseuse	hairdresser
Geschäftsführer/in	manager
Geschäftsmann	businessman
Geschäftsfrau	businesswoman
Hausfrau	housewife
Hausmann	househusband
Ingenieur	engineer
Journalist/in	journalist
Kellner/in	waiter/waitress
Koch/Köchin	cook
Krankenpfleger	male nurse
Krankenschwester/	female nurse
Krankenpflegerin	
Lehrer/in	teacher
Metzger/in	butcher
Pilot/in	pilot
Polizist/in	police officer
Rechtsanwalt/anwältin	lawyer
Sänger/in	singer
Schauspieler/in	actor/actress
Verkäufer/in	sales person

Examples of what you may hear:

Mein Vater ist Geschäftsmann. My father is a businessman.
Meine Mutter ist Lehrerin. My mother is a teacher.
Mein Bruder ist arbeitslos. My brother is unemployed.

Sometimes you may not hear the person's profession, but simply the place of work, e.g.

Er/Sie arbeitet:

in einer	**Bibliothek**	library
	Fabrik	factory
	Schule	school
in einem	**Büro**	office
	Laden	shop
	Krankenhaus	hospital

Part-Time Jobs

der Nebenjob/der Teilzeitjob   part-time job

Ich gehe bei meinen Nachbarn babysitten. I babysit for my neighbours.
Ich arbeite: I work:
  in einer Tankstelle   at a petrol station
  in einem Supermarkt   in a supermarket
  auf einem Bauernhof   on a farm
  in einem Geschäft   in a shop
  an der Kasse   at the check-out
Ich bediene die Kunden.   I serve the customers.

Money

Ich verdiene sieben Euro/ I earn €7 an hour.
  7€ pro Stunde.
Ich bekomme zehn Euro I get €10 pocket money a week.
  Taschengeld die Woche.
Meine Oma schenkt mir Geld My granny gives me money for
  zum Geburtstag. my birthday.
Ich *gebe* mein Geld für I spend my money on clothes.
  Klamotten *aus*.
Ich kaufe Geschenke für I buy presents for my friends.
  meine Freunde.

Ich spare für einen Computer.	I'm saving for a computer.
für die Ferien	for the holidays
für ein neues Fahrrad	for a new bicycle
Das Geld reicht mir nicht.	The money is not enough for me.
Ich brauche viel Geld für	I need a lot of money for the weekend.
das Wochenende.	

Adjectives:

895, 188/YA 438

arm	poor
reich	rich
großzügig	generous

PENPALS AND EXCHANGES

Penpals

Ich habe einen Brieffreund/eine Brieffreundin.   I have a penpal.

Some examples of where penpals may come from:

Belgien	Belgium	**Norwegen**	Norway
Dänemark	Denmark	**Österreich**	Austria
England	England	**Polen**	Poland
Frankreich	France	**Schottland**	Scotland
Griechenland	Greece	**die Schweiz**	Switzerland
Großbritannien	Great Britain	**Spanien**	Spain
Holland	Holland	**die Türkei**	Turkey
Irland	Ireland	**Ungarn**	Hungary

Exchanges

Ich mache einen Schüleraustausch/ Austausch.	I'm doing an exchange.
Wir *holen* meine Austauschpartnerin am Flughafen *ab*.	We are collecting my exchange partner at the airport.
Sie fliegt am vierzehnten Juni nach München.	She is flying to Munich on 14 June.
Er *kommt* um vier Uhr am Bahnhof *an*.	He is arriving at the station at 4 o'clock.
Ich *freue mich auf* ihren/seinen Besuch.	I'm looking forward to her/his visit.

At the train station

The following phrases may be heard in dialogue at a train station ('am Bahnhof').

Was kostet eine Fahrkarte nach Freiburg, bitte?	How much is a ticket to Freiburg, please?
Zweimal nach München, bitte, einfach.	Two single tickets to Munich, please.
Einmal nach Frankfurt hin und zurück./Eine Rückfahrkarte nach Frankfurt.	One return ticket to Frankfurt.
Möchten Sie einen Platz reservieren?	Would you like to reserve a seat?
Muss ich umsteigen?	Do I have to change trains?
Von welchem Gleis fährt der Zug ab?	What platform does the train leave from?

Wo fährt der Zug ab?	Where does the train leave from?
Wann/Um wie viel Uhr fährt der Zug?	When /At what time does the train leave?
Der Zug kommt am Gleis sieben an.	The train is arriving at Platform 7.
Der Zug hat zwanzig Minuten Verspätung.	The train is 20 minutes late.

Other Modes of Transport

das Auto/der Wagen	car	**das Fahrrad**	bicycle
die Straßenbahn	tram	**das Motorrad**	motorbike
der Bus	bus	**das Flugzeug**	plane
die U-Bahn	underground train	**die Fähre**	ferry

Ich fahre mit dem Auto/mit dem Bus zur Schule.	I go by car/bus to school.
Sie fährt mit der Straßenbahn/ der U-Bahn in die Stadt.	She goes to town by tram/underground.
Ich gehe zu Fuß.	I walk.

The journey

Wie war die Reise?	What was the journey like?
Die Reise war sehr angenehm.	The journey was very pleasant.
Die Überfahrt war stürmisch.	The crossing was stormy.
Wie lange dauert die Fahrt?	How long does the journey take?
Die Fahrt dauert eine Stunde.	The journey takes an hour.
Der Flug dauert zweieinhalb Stunden.	The flight lasts two and a half hours.
Gute Reise!	Have a good trip!

Adjectives:

German	English	German	English
spät	late	**langsam**	slow
früh	early	**schnell**	fast
pünktlich	punctual	**seekrank**	seasick

The following is a transcript of a dialogue from the 2001 Listening test.

Am Bahnhof

Bitte schön?

Tag. Ich möchte gerne eine Fahrkarte nach Berlin, bitte.

Hin und zurück?

Ja, hin und zurück, bitte. Ich möchte am Freitag nach Berlin und am Sonntag zurück nach Kassel.

Wann möchten Sie fahren, morgens oder . . . ?

Am Freitagmorgen, um halb neun, bitte, und am Sonntagabend um 18 Uhr zurück.

Das kostet 170 Mark für die Fahrkarte plus 12 Mark Platzreservierung, also zusammen 182 Mark.*

182 Mark. Vielen Dank. Tschüss!

Auf Wiedersehen!

* pre-euro test

IN TOWN

Buildings and Other Features

der

Bahnhof	railway station	**Blumenladen**	flower shop
Hauptbahnhof	main station	**Heimwerkerladen**	DIY shop
Dom	cathedral	**Musikladen**	music shop
Flughafen	airport	**Schreibwarenladen**	stationery shop
Fluss	river	**Spielwarenladen**	toy shop
Gemüsehändler	greengrocer	**Supermarkt**	supermarket
Imbissstand	snack stall	**Marktplatz**	market square
Laden	shop	**Tiergarten**	zoo

die

Altstadt	old town	**Fußgängerzone**	pedestrian area
Apotheke	pharmacy	**Jugendherberge**	youth hostel
Bäckerei	bakery	**Kirche**	church
Bank	bank	**Kneipe**	pub
Bibliothek/ Bücherei	library	**Konditorei**	cake shop
Brücke	bridge	**Kunstgalerie**	art gallery
Buchhandlung	book shop	**Metzgerei**	butcher's shop
Burg	castle	**Polizeiwache**	police station
Bushaltestelle	bus stop	**Post**	post office
Drogerie	chemist's shop	**Schule**	school
Eisdiele	ice-cream parlour	**Tankstelle**	petrol station
Fabrik	factory	**U-Bahn-Station**	underground station

das

Einkaufszentrum	shopping centre	**Reisebüro**	travel agency
Geschäft	shop	**Schloss**	castle
Möbelgeschäft	furniture shop	**Schwimmbad**	swimming pool
Modegeschäft	boutique	**Freibad**	outdoor pool
Jugendzentrum	youth centre	**Hallenbad**	indoor pool
Kaufhaus	department store	**Sportzentrum**	sport centre
Kino	cinema	**Stadion**	stadium
Krankenhaus	hospital	**Theater**	theatre
Museum	museum	**Verkehrsamt**	tourist office
Parkhaus	multi-storey car park	**Warenhaus**	department store
Rathaus	town hall		

Directions

Questions and phrases frequently heard in Section B of the Listening test:

Wie komme ich zum Schwimmbad/ zur Bibliothek?	How do I get to the swimming pool/library?
Wo ist die Post, bitte?	Where is the post office, please?
Entschuldigung. Ist hier in der Nähe eine Bank?	Excuse me. Is there a bank near here?
Ich bin hier fremd. Ich suche den Bahnhof.	I'm a stranger here. I'm looking for the train station.

Remember!

LINKS   RECHTS

GERADEAUS

Nehmen Sie die dritte Straße links.	Take the third street left.
Nehmen Sie die erste Straße rechts.	Take the first street right.
Gehen Sie hier geradeaus.	Go straight on.
Biegen **Sie nach links** *ab*.	Turn left.
Überqueren Sie die Straße.	Cross the street.

um die Ecke	around the corner
an der Ampel	at the lights
über die Brücke	over the bridge
bis zur Kreuzung	as far as the crossroads
am Fluss entlang	along the river
an der Schule vorbei	past the school
gegenüber vom Rathaus	opposite the Town Hall
hinter der Kirche	behind the church
neben der Kunstgalerie	beside the art gallery

ganz einfach	quite simple
nicht weit	not far
ziemlich weit	quite far
zehn Minuten zu Fuß	ten minutes on foot
nach zweihundert Metern	after 200 metres

Adjectives:

leicht/einfach	easy		**eng**	narrow
kompliziert	complicated		**nah**	near
breit	wide		**weit**	far

The following is a transcript of a dialogue from the 2003 Listening test.

In der Stadt

Entschuldigung, könnten Sie mir helfen? Ich bin hier fremd und suche das Schwimmbad.

Moment mal – das Freibad oder das Hallenbad?

Das Freibad.

Also, gehen Sie hier geradeaus und dann die erste Straße rechts, an der Kirche vorbei, bis zum Fluss. Da sehen Sie dann das Freibad, direkt am Fluss.

Okay, geradeaus, erste Straße rechts, an der Kirche vorbei, bis zum Fluss. Vielen Dank.

Meeting Points

der Treffpunkt	meeting point
Wo treffen wir uns?	Where shall we meet?
Vor dem Kino.	In front of the cinema.
Am Schwimmbad.	At the swimming pool.
In der Eisdiele.	In the ice-cream parlour.
Wann treffen wir uns?	When shall we meet?
Um zehn <u>vor</u> acht.	At ten to eight.
Um <u>halb</u> eins.	At half past twelve.
<u>**Um vier Uhr.**</u>	At four o'clock.

Lost and Found

<u>**verloren**</u>	lost
<u>**gefunden**</u>	found
das Fundbüro	lost and found office
eine Belohnung	reward
Ich möchte einen Verlust/einen Diebstahl melden.	I'd like to report a loss/a robbery.

Ich habe mein Portemonnaie im Café liegen lassen.	I left my purse behind in the café.
Wir haben unseren Hund verloren.	We lost our dog.
Er hat seine Schlüssel verloren.	He lost his keys.
Achtung! Eine wichtige Durchsage.	Attention! An important announcement.
Peters Eltern suchen ihren kleinen Sohn.	Peter's parents are looking for their little son.
Sie warten an der Information.	They are waiting at the information desk.
Die vierjährige Maria sucht ihre Mutter.	Four-year-old Maria is looking for her mother.

NUMBERS

1	eins	15	fünfzehn	90	neunzig
2	zwei	16	sechzehn	99	neunundneunzig
	(sometimes 'zwo')	17	siebzehn	100	hundert
3	drei	18	achtzehn	101	hunderteins
4	vier	19	neunzehn	102	hundertzwei
5	fünf	20	zwanzig	200	zweihundert
6	sechs	21	einundzwanzig	201	zweihunderteins
7	sieben	22	zweiundzwanzig	202	zweihundertzwei
8	acht	30	dreißig	300	dreihundert
9	neun	31	einunddreißig	1000	tausend
10	zehn	40	vierzig		eine Million
11	elf	50	fünfzig		
12	zwölf	60	sechzig		
13	dreizehn	70	siebzig		
14	vierzehn	80	achtzig		

Remember! In German numbers the units always come first, e.g.

einundvierzig = one and forty (41)
dreiundachtzig = three and eighty (83).

der/die/das erste	the first	achte	eighth
zweite	second	neunte	ninth
dritte	third	zehnte	tenth
vierte	fourth	siebzehnte	seventeenth
fünfte	fifth	zwanzigste	twentieth
sechste	sixth	einundzwanzigste	twenty-first
siebte	seventh	dreißigste	thirtieth

Phone numbers

You will normally hear phone numbers in double digits, e.g.
neunundsiebzig einunddreißig vierundachtzig = 79 31 84.

The prefix (Vorwahl) is generally given in single digits, e.g.
null vier fünf eins = 0451.

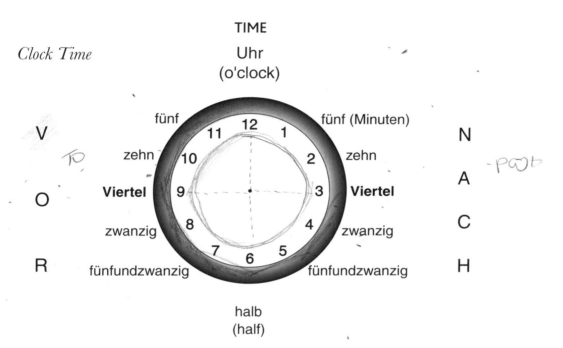

TIME

Uhr
(o'clock)

Clock Time

Wie viel Uhr ist es?/Wie spät ist es? What time is it?

Es ist ein Uhr.	It is one o'clock.
Viertel vor eins	a quarter to one
zwei Uhr	two o'clock
Viertel nach sieben	a quarter past seven
fünf nach drei	five past three
zwanzig vor zehn	twenty to ten
Mittag	midday
Mitternacht	midnight

Note: It is very important to recognise how 'half' is expressed when telling the time in German. Whereas in English 'half six' means half *past* six, i.e. 6.30, in German 'halb sechs' means half an hour *before* six, i.e. 5.30.

Can you work these out?

halb elf _____10.30_____   halb vier _____5.30_____

halb eins _____1.30_____   halb neun _____9.30_____

um **sieben Uhr**	at 7.00
um **halb zehn**	at 9.30
gegen **acht Uhr**	around 8.00
gegen **Mittag**	around midday

Note: You will not hear the terms 'a.m.' and 'p.m.' in German. So how do you tell the difference?

8 a.m. = **acht Uhr morgens/vormittags**

8 p.m. = **acht Uhr abends**

3 p.m. = **drei Uhr nachmittags**

Of course, if you are listening to official times, for example for trains or film showings, the digital or 24-hour system is used:

dreizehn Uhr fünfundzwanzig	13.25
achtzehn Uhr fünfzehn	18.15
neunzehn Uhr dreißig	19.30
zweiundzwanzig Uhr fünfundvierzig	22.45

Days of the Week

Montag	Monday
Dienstag	Tuesday
Mittwoch	Wednesday
Donnerstag	Thursday
Freitag	Friday
Samstag/Sonnabend	Saturday
Sonntag	Sunday

heute	today
gestern	yesterday
vorgestern	the day before yesterday
morgen	tomorrow
übermorgen	the day after tomorrow
heute Nachmittag	this afternoon

gestern Vormittag	yesterday morning
morgen Abend	tomorrow evening
am Dienstagabend	on Tuesday evening
am Samstagnachmittag	on Saturday afternoon

Months and Dates

Januar	January	Juli	July
Februar	February	August	August
März	March	September	September
April	April	Oktober	October
Mai	May	November	November
Juni	June	Dezember	December

Der Wievielte ist heute?/Den Wievielten haben wir heute?	What date is today?
Heute ist der erste Mai./Heute haben wir den ersten Mai.	Today is the first of May.
am **fünften Mai**	on 5 May
vom **achten** *bis* **zum zwölften Februar**	from 8 to 12 February

(Refer to NUMBERS section on p. 26 for first, second, third, etc.)

neunzehnhundertneunundneunzig	1999
zweitausendfünf	2005
im Jahre zweitausendsechs	in the year 2006
im neunzehnten Jahrhundert	in the nineteenth century
im einundzwanzigsten Jahrhundert	in the twenty-first century

Seasons

die vier Jahreszeiten	the four seasons
der Frühling	spring
der Sommer	summer
der Herbst	autumn
der Winter	winter
Meine Lieblingsjahreszeit ist der Herbst. Sommer	My favourite season is autumn.

Other Time Phrases

ab und zu	now and then	**letzten Sommer**	last summer
oft/häufig	often/frequently	**letzte Woche**	last week
immer	always	**jeden Tag**	every day
nie	never	**jedes Wochenende**	every weekend
manchmal	sometimes	**fast jeden Abend**	nearly every evening
selten	seldom	**nächstes Jahr**	next year
stundenlang	for hours	**nächsten Montag**	next Monday
am Wochenende	at the weekend	**diese Woche**	this week
in den Ferien	in the holidays	**dieses Jahr**	this year
während der Pause	during the break	**bald**	soon

Note: It is important to recognise how German expresses 'ago': The word 'vor' is used *before* the time phrase. In English we say 'two years *ago*'. In German that is '*vor* zwei Jahren':

Wir sind vor einem Jahr umgezogen.   We moved house a year ago.

What do the following mean?

vor einer Woche ___for one week___

vor einem Monat ___for one month___

vor zehn Minuten ___for ten minutes___

For/since

In German the word 'seit' is used to say '*for* how long' or '*since* when' something has been going on:

Ich lerne *seit* drei Jahren Deutsch. I have been learning German *for* three years.

Wir wohnen *seit* 1995 in Düsseldorf. We have been living in Düsseldorf *since* 1995.

Try these!

For or since?

seit zwei Stunden ___for___

seit dem elften Dezember ___since___

seit Viertel nach fünf ___since___

seit drei Monaten ___for___

Festivals

Silvester	New Year's Eve
Neujahr	New Year's Day
der Fasching/die Fastnacht/	carnival in different German-speaking
der Karneval	regions
Rosenmontag	Monday before Shrove Tuesday
Faschingsdienstag	Shrove Tuesday
sich verkleiden	to wear fancy dress
der Umzug	parade/procession
Pfingsten	Whitsun
Ostern	Easter
Aschermittwoch	Ash Wednesday
Karfreitag	Good Friday
Ostersonntag	Easter Sunday
der Osterhase	Easter bunny
die Ostereier	Easter eggs
die Osterferien	Easter holidays

Weihnachten	Christmas
der Weihnachtsmann	Father Christmas
der Weihnachtsbaum	Christmas tree
der Tannenbaum	fir tree
die Weihnachtslieder	Christmas carols
das Geschenk/die Geschenke	present/presents
die Einladung	invitation
Heiligabend	Christmas Eve
die Gans	goose
der Truthahn	turkey
Sankt Nikolaus	Saint Nicholas: gives presents to children on 6 December
das Christkind	the baby Jesus/the Christ child

SEEKING ACCOMMODATION

Hotel

Haben Sie ein Zimmer frei?	Do you have a room free?
Wir haben ein Einzelzimmer mit Bad.	We have a single room with a bath.
Ich möchte ein Doppelzimmer mit Dusche, bitte.	I would like a double room with a shower.
Was kostet eine Nacht mit Frühstück?	How much is one night with breakfast?

Youth Hostel

Haben Sie Platz frei?	Do you have any vacancies?
Braucht ihr Bettwäsche?	Do you need bedlinen?
Ich habe einen Schlafsack.	I have a sleeping bag.
Welche Mahlzeiten möchtet ihr?	What meals would you like?
Die Mädchenschlafräume sind im zweiten Stock.	The girls' dormitories are on the second floor.
Sie finden den Speisesaal im Keller.	You will find the dining room in the basement.

Campsite

Ich möchte einen Zeltplatz, bitte. I would like a place for a tent, please.
Wir wollen drei Nächte bleiben. We want to stay three nights.

The following is a transcript of a dialogue from the 2003 Listening test.

In der Jugendherberge

Guten Abend.
Guten Abend. Haben Sie noch Platz frei?
Ja, für wie viele Personen?
Für fünf Personen: für zwei Mädchen und drei Jungen, bitte.
Für wie viele Nächte?
Für vier Nächte.
Okay, das geht. Braucht ihr Bettwäsche?
Nein, danke, wir haben Schlafsäcke dabei.
In Ordnung. Die Mädchen sind im Erdgeschoss, in Zimmer 8, und die Jungen sind im zweiten Stock, in Zimmer 25.
Also, die Mädchen hier im Erdgeschoss in Zimmer 8 und wir Jungen . . .
Die Jungen oben im zweiten Stock, Zimmer 25.
Eine letzte Frage noch: Wo ist der Tischtennisraum, bitte?
Der Tischtennisraum ist unten im Keller, aber er ist im Moment leider geschlossen, weil das Fenster kaputt ist.

German Alphabet

In a telephone conversation you may hear a request to spell a surname, e.g. when someone is booking accommodation. You should revise carefully the sounds of the letters in German. Ideally you should do this by listening, but here is a rough written guide to the way they are pronounced.

A	ah	G	gay	M	em	S	ess	Y	upsilon
B	bay	H	hah	N	en	T	tay	Z	tset
C	tsay	I	ee	O	oh	U	oo		
D	day	J	yot	P	pay	V	fow		
E	ay	K	kah	Q	koo	W	vay		
F	ef	L	el	R	air	X	ix		

Note: As you know, the sounds of the three broad vowels A, O and U may be narrowed in German by the use of the *Umlaut* (Ä, Ö, Ü).

WEATHER

Wie ist das Wetter?	What's the weather like?
Die Sonne scheint.	The sun is shining.
Es regnet.	It is raining.
Es hagelt.	There are hailstones.
Es schneit.	It is snowing.
Es friert.	It is freezing.
Es donnert.	It is thundering.
Es blitzt.	There is lightning.
Es ist schön und warm.	It is nice and warm.
Es ist sonnig und heiß.	It is sunny and hot.
Es ist kalt und windig.	It is cold and windy.
Es ist kühl und nebelig.	It is cool and misty.
Es ist wolkig/bewölkt.	It is cloudy.
Es ist bedeckt.	It is overcast.

Other weather phrases:

der Sturm	storm
das Gewitter	thunderstorm
die Temperatur	temperature
bei gutem Wetter	in good weather
bei schlechtem Wetter	in bad weather
der Wetterbericht	weather report
die Wettervorhersage	weather forecast

Adjectives:

furchtbar	terrible
heiter	bright
trocken	dry
stürmisch	stormy
stark	strong
starker Wind	strong wind
schwach	weak/light

Note: Weather reports usually include reference to geographical location. You may hear:

im Norden	in the north
im Süden	in the south
im Osten	in the east
im Westen	in the west

or combinations such as **im Südwesten** or **im Nordosten**.

ILLNESS AND ACCIDENTS

Illness

Wie geht's?	How are you?
Mir geht's gut, danke.	I'm fine, thank you.
Ich fühle mich nicht wohl.	I don't feel well.
Ich habe Kopfschmerzen/Kopfweh.	I have a headache.
Halsschmerzen	sore throat
Bauchschmerzen/Magenschmerzen	tummy ache
Zahnschmerzen	toothache
Rückenschmerzen	backache
Ich schwitze.	I'm sweating.
Ich habe Fieber.	I have a temperature.
Ich habe mich erbrochen.	I vomited.
Ich bin erkältet./Ich habe eine Erkältung./Ich habe einen Schnupfen.	I've got a cold.
Ich habe die Grippe.	I have the flu.
Ich habe Husten.	I have a cough.
Mir ist warm.	I am hot.
Mir ist kalt.	I am cold.
Soll ich den Arzt anrufen?	Should I ring the doctor?

At the Doctor or in the Pharmacy

Ich habe einen Termin.	I have an appointment.
Was fehlt Ihnen?	What is wrong with you?
Nehmen Sie diese Tabletten zweimal täglich.	Take these tablets twice a day.
Legen Sie sich ins Bett!	Go to bed.
Sie sollten möglichst viel trinken.	You should drink as much as possible.
Ich habe einen Sonnenbrand.	I am sunburnt.

Haben Sie etwas gegen Ohrenschmerzen?	Have you got something for an earache?
Nehmen Sie das Nasenspray alle zwei Stunden.	Take the nose spray every two hours.
Seit wann tut das weh?	How long has it been sore?
Mach den Mund auf!	Open your mouth.
Du solltest gesund essen. Weniger Süßigkeiten!	You should eat healthily. Fewer sweet things!

Accidents

Was ist passiert?	What happened?
Was ist los?	What is wrong?
Ich habe einen Unfall gehabt.	I've had an accident.
Ich habe mir das Bein gebrochen.	I have broken my leg.
Ich habe mir das Fußgelenk verstaucht.	I have sprained my ankle.
Hast du dir die Hand verletzt?	Have you injured your hand?
Ich habe mir die Hand verbrannt.	I have burnt my hand.
Ich habe mir in den Finger geschnitten.	I've cut my finger.
Sie ist vom Fahrrad gefallen.	She fell off her bicycle.
Ihr Knie tut weh.	Her knee hurts.
Gute Besserung!	Get well soon!

The following is a transcript of a dialogue from the 2002 Listening test.

Uli hat einen Unfall

Hallo, Martin, hier ist die Sabine.

Mensch, Sabine, wie geht's? Wir treffen uns heute Abend bei Uli, oder?

Eben nicht, deshalb rufe ich dich an. Wir treffen uns heute Abend nicht bei Uli, denn er liegt im Krankenhaus. Er hat einen Unfall gehabt.

Einen Unfall? Er ist im Krankenhaus? Was ist passiert? Ist er verletzt?

Er ist vom Fahrrad gefallen und hat sich den rechten Arm gebrochen und den Rücken verletzt. Ich will ihn morgen im Krankenhaus besuchen. Willst du mit?

Klar will ich mit. Wann und wo treffen wir uns?

Morgen um Viertel nach zwei an der Bushaltestelle vor dem Krankenhaus.

In Ordnung. Morgen um Viertel nach zwei an der Bushaltestelle. Bis dann, tschüss.

CLOTHES

die Kleidung/Kleider/Klamotten clothes

der Anzug	suit	**das Kleid**	dress
der Badeanzug	bathing suit	**die Krawatte**	tie
der Schlafanzug	pyjamas	**der Mantel**	coat
der Trainingsanzug	tracksuit	**der Bademantel**	bathrobe
die Bluse	blouse	**der Regenmantel**	raincoat
der Gürtel	belt	**die Mütze**	cap
die Handschuhe	gloves	**die Pantoffel**	slipper
das Hemd	shirt	**der Pullover/Pulli**	jumper
das Fußballhemd	football jersey	**der Rock**	skirt
das Nachthemd	night shirt	**die Sandalen**	sandals
das Unterhemd	vest	**der Schal**	scarf
die Hose	trousers	**der Schlips**	tie
die Badehose	bathing togs	**die Schuhe**	shoes
die Strumpfhose	tights	**die Stiefel**	boots
der Hut	hat	**die Gummistiefel**	rubber boots
die Jacke	jacket	**das T-Shirt**	T-shirt
die Lederjacke	leather jacket		

Ich trage gern sportliche Klamotten.	I like wearing sporty clothes.
In Deutschland trägt man keine Schuluniform.	They don't wear a school uniform in Germany.
Ich *ziehe* mir eine Jacke *an*.	I put on a jacket.
Er *zieht* sich nach der Schule *um*.	He gets changed after school.

Buying clothes

In der Modeabteilung	*In the fashion department*
Darf ich diesen Rock anprobieren, bitte?	May I try on this skirt, please?
Die Umkleidekabine ist dort drüben.	The changing room is over there.
Welche Größe haben Sie?	What size do you take?
Größe achtunddreißig.	Size 38.

Haben Sie das in Groß/ Medium/Klein?	Do you have that in large/medium/ small?
Das Hemd gefällt mir.	I like the shirt.
Darf ich diesen Pulli umtauschen, bitte?	May I exchange this jumper, please?
Ich nehme diesen Schal, bitte.	I'll take this scarf, please.
Das Kleid passt dir nicht.	The dress does not fit you.
Es ist zu groß/klein/lang/ kurz/eng.	It is too big/small/long/short/tight.
Die Farbe steht dir.	The colour suits you.
Blau steht mir nicht.	Blue does not suit me.

Other Colours

braun	brown		**rot**	red
gelb	yellow		**schwarz**	black
grau	grey		**violett**	purple
grün	green		**weiß**	white
lila	lilac		**bunt**	multicoloured
rosa	pink			

Adjectives:

altmodisch	old-fashioned	**teuer**	expensive
schick	trendy	**preiswert/preisgünstig**	inexpensive
hübsch	pretty	**gepunktet**	spotted
hässlich	horrible, ugly	**gestreift**	striped
billig	cheap	**kariert**	checked

SHOPPING

Quantities

ein Kilo Äpfel	a kilo of apples
fünfhundert Gramm Tomaten	500 g tomatoes
ein Bund Karotten	a bunch of carrots
ein Liter Milch	a litre of milk
eine Dose Limonade	a can of lemonade
eine Flasche Wein	a bottle of wine
ein Glas Kirschen	a jar of cherries
eine Schachtel Streichhölzer	a box of matches
eine Packung Kekse	a packet of biscuits
eine Tüte Bonbons	a bag of sweets
eine Tafel Schokolade	a bar of chocolate
ein Strauß Blumen	a bunch of flowers

Other Items

der Schmuck	jewellery
die Geschenkartikel	gift items
die Süßigkeiten	confectionery
die Schminke	make-up
die Seife	soap
die Zahnpasta	toothpaste
das Parfüm	perfume
die Taschentücher	tissues
die Schreibwaren	stationery
die Bücher	books
die Zeitschriften	magazines
die Zeitungen	newspapers
das Handy	mobile phone

In the Post Office

Was kostet ein Brief nach Irland, bitte?	How much does a letter to Ireland cost?
Was kostet eine Postkarte nach Frankreich?	How much does a postcard to France cost?
Zwei Briefmarken zu sechzig Cent.	Two stamps at 60 cent.
Ich möchte dieses Paket nach Österreich schicken.	I would like to send this parcel to Austria.

Other Useful Phrases

Kann ich Ihnen helfen?	Can I help you?
Sonst noch etwas?	Anything else?
Was kosten die Ohrringe?	How much are the earrings?
Ich suche ein Geschenk für meinen Vater.	I'm looking for a present for my father.
Wo ist die Sportabteilung?	Where is the sports department?
Zahlen Sie an der Kasse!	Pay at the cash desk.
Es ist mir zu teuer.	It is too expensive for me.
Haben Sie etwas Billigeres?	Have you anything cheaper?
Sonderangebot!	Special offer!
Ende August ist Sommerschlussverkauf.	The summer sale is at the end of August.

FOOD AND DRINK

Meals

die Mahlzeiten	meals
das Frühstück	breakfast
das Mittagessen	lunch
das Abendessen/Abendbrot	evening meal

Fruit

das Obst	fruit	**die Birne**	pear
die Ananas	pineapple	**die Erdbeere**	strawberry
der Apfel/die Äpfel	apple/apples	**die Himbeere**	raspberry
die Apfelsine/Orange	orange	**die Kirsche**	cherry
die Aprikose	apricot	**die Melone**	melon
die Banane	banana	**die Pampelmuse**	grapefruit

| der Pfirsich | peach | die Traube | grape |
| die Pflaume | plum | die Zitrone | lemon |

Vegetables

das Gemüse	vegetables	der Kopfsalat	lettuce
der Blumenkohl	cauliflower	die Paprikaschote	pepper
die Bohnen	beans	die Pilze/Champignons	mushrooms
die Erbsen	peas	der Rosenkohl	Brussels sprouts
die Gurke	cucumber	der Spargel	asparagus
die Karotte/Möhre	carrot	der Spinat	spinach
der Knoblauch	garlic	die Tomate	tomato
der Kohl	cabbage	die Zwiebel	onion

Meat

das Fleisch	meat	die Salami	salami
das Hackfleisch	minced meat	das Hähnchen	chicken
das Lammfleisch	lamb		
das Rindfleisch	beef	der Fisch	fish
das Schweinefleisch	pork	die Forelle	trout
das Schnitzel	veal/pork cutlet	der Lachs	salmon
der Schinken	ham	der Thunfisch	tuna
der Speck	bacon		
die Wurst	sausage		
der Aufschnitt	cold meat slices		

Dairy Products

die Butter	butter	die Margarine	margarine
die Milch	milk	die Sahne	cream
der Käse	cheese	der Joghurt	yoghurt

Bread and Cereals

das Brot	bread	die Haferflocken	porridge oats
das Brötchen	bread roll	das Müsli	muesli
das Schwarzbrot	brown rye bread	der Reis	rice
das Weißbrot	white bread		
das Vollkornbrot	wholemeal bread		

Other Food Items

der Eintopf	stew	**die Kekse**	biscuits
die Marmelade	jam	**die Nudeln**	noodles/pasta
der Honig	honey	**die Kartoffelchips/**	crisps
		Chips	

Drinks

die Getränke	drinks	**der Kakao**	cocoa
das Wasser	water	**der Saft**	juice
das Mineralwasser/	mineral water	**der Fruchtsaft**	fruit juice
der Sprudel		**der Apfelsaft**	apple juice
die Milch	milk	**der Orangensaft**	orange juice
der Tee	tea	**das Bier**	beer
der Kaffee	coffee	**der Wein**	wine

Eating out

Am Schnellimbiss

Was darf es sein?/
   Was möchten Sie?
Einmal Schaschlik mit Currysoße.
Zweimal Bratwurst mit Senf.
Eine große/kleine Portion
   Pommes/Pommes frites.

At the snack stall

What would you like?

One kebab with curry sauce.
Two sausages with mustard.
A large/small portion of chips.

Im Café/In der Eisdiele

In the café/ice-cream parlour

Ein Stück Käsekuchen mit
   Sahne, bitte.
Ein Stück Himbeertorte ohne
   Sahne.
Zweimal Apfelstrudel.
Zwei Stück Schwarzwälder-
   kirschtorte.
Einmal Schokoladeneis.
Ein gemischtes Eis.
Einmal Tee mit Zitrone.
Zwei Tassen Kaffee.
Ein Kännchen Kaffee.
Ich möchte eine Schokolade.
Zahlen, bitte.
Zusammen oder getrennt?

A piece of cheese cake with cream,
   please.
A piece of raspberry flan without
   cream.
Two apple strudels/pastries.
Two pieces of Black Forest gateau.

One chocolate ice cream.
One mixed ice cream.
One tea with lemon.
Two cups of coffee.
One pot of coffee.
I would like a hot chocolate.
The bill, please.
Together or separate?

Im Restaurant

In the restaurant

die Speisekarte	menu
die Vorspeise	starter
die Hauptspeise/das Hauptgericht	main course
die Nachspeise/der Nachtisch/	
das Dessert	dessert
der Kellner/die Kellnerin	waiter/waitress
Herr Ober!	Waiter!

Other useful vocabulary:

Das schmeckt!	That tastes good!
Ich habe Hunger./Ich bin hungrig.	I'm hungry.
Ich habe Durst./Ich bin durstig.	I'm thirsty.
Ich bin satt.	I'm full.

Adjectives:

lecker	delicious
süß	sweet
sauer	sour
frisch	fresh

Recipes

das Rezept	recipe
die Zutaten	ingredients
zubereiten	to prepare
das Mehl	flour
die Butter	butter
der Zucker	sugar
die Rosinen	raisins
das Ei/die Eier	egg/s
der Zimt	cinnamon
die Mandeln	almonds
die Nüsse	nuts
das Backpulver	baking powder
das Salz	salt
der Pfeffer	pepper
das Öl	oil
der Essig	vinegar
die Gewürze	spices
das Basilikum	basil
geriebener Käse	grated cheese
ein Teelöffel	a teaspoon
ein Esslöffel	a table spoon
zweihundert Gramm	200 grams
hundertfünfzig Gramm	150 grams
ein viertel Liter	a quarter of a litre
eine Prise Salz	a pinch of salt
Guten Appetit!	Enjoy your meal!

2. READING COMPREHENSION

(100 marks)

This part of the exam tests your comprehension (understanding) of written German. You will already have completed the Listening Comprehension test and will have plenty of German in your head. Most of your time here will be spent reading. There is no choice involved as *all questions must be answered*.

There are seven sections (A–G) in the Reading Comprehension test with a variety of material in German, ranging from short texts (signs, notices, small ads, etc.) to longer passages. This part of the book shows you how to go about answering the Reading Comprehension questions. In each of the seven sections headed A–G you will find

    (a) a sample question with guided answers

    (b) a 'Test Yourself' question

    (c) a Past Exam question.

In the sample question with guided answers you are shown how to approach the text and given tips on how to answer in such a way as to maximise your marks.

You may then test your skills in the 'Test Yourself' and Past Exam questions, answers to which are at the end of the Reading Comprehension section (pages 93–98).

Exam Tips

1. You should start this section after you finish the Listening Comprehension test. You could, of course, choose to do the Written Expression first, but this is not recommended. It is a much better idea to do this section first as it involves reading a lot of German, which will refresh the language in your mind.

2. As this section is worth more marks than the Written Expression, it should be given a little more time. You should spend roughly an hour here reading, answering and checking your answers. Obviously the longer passages (F and G) will need more reading time than the earlier ones.

3. Remember that this is *Reading* Comprehension. It is a good idea to read the questions first as you will get an indication of what the text is about. Do not underestimate the need to read and reread the text itself until you have a clear understanding of the content.

4. It is not necessary to understand every word in a text to be able to answer the questions fully and correctly. So, don't panic if you see a word you don't understand.

5. Before you write an answer, make sure that you have read the question carefully and that you have chosen the correct detail, number of details and source of information (paragraph number, lines, box) where this information is given.

6. Write your answers clearly and in the correct spaces provided on the paper. If more than one line is provided, you probably need to write more than a word or two. Always be sure to give a *full* answer.

7. It is very important to check your answers carefully. This does not mean simply reading what you have written. You should read each question, check the source of your answer in the text and make sure that you have included all the necessary information.

VIEL ERFOLG!

Section A

There are three questions in this first section. Each question asks you to choose the correct word or expression among four given.

SAMPLE QUESTION

1. You want to buy a **toy** in a German store. Which word do you use? **Rewrite** the chosen word.

SPIELPLATZ	SPIEL	SPIELZEUG	KINDERBEKLEIDUNG

How to choose? Start by examining each word carefully. You probably know some of these words already. You will recognise 'Spiel' from the word 'spielen' (to play) or perhaps from 'Fußballspiel'. The fourth word looks very different, but you should not jump to the conclusion that it is the one you need. Break it down and you find 'Kinder' (children) and 'bekleidung' (clothing), so this is obviously not the word for a toy. Which of the three remaining words could it be? 'Spielplatz'? You know 'platz' as in 'Ist dieser Platz frei?' (Is this place free?). 'Spiel' is a game or a match, as in 'Fußballspiel'. Combine 'Spiel' with 'platz' and you have a 'place for playing' or a playground.

So you are left with 'Spielzeug'. Although you may not know the word, you have worked through the other options intelligently and chosen the correct word. 'Spielzeug' means a 'play thing' or a toy.

2. You are leaving a building in Germany. Which sign indicates the **exit?** **Rewrite** the chosen word.

AUSGANG	EINGANG	DURCHGANG	AUSSTELLUNG

Here again, you will probably know some of the words. However, it is important not to rush your answer. Examine the prefixes 'aus', 'ein', 'durch' for clues. Which one means 'out'? 'Aus'. So now you are left with 50/50! You have rejected 'Eingang' and 'Durchgang' and must now choose between 'Aus*gang*' and

'Aus*stellung*'. If you do not know the word for exit, make an intelligent choice. You will have heard the form of the verb 'gehen' (to go) in the past tense, as in 'Er ist gegangen'. So 'Ausgang' must have something to do with going out. It is the correct choice.

The meanings of the other words in this example are: 'Eingang' (entrance), 'Durchgang' (passageway), 'Ausstellung' (exhibition).

Note: Beware of German words which may look similar to English. These may be 'false friends' which are not to be relied on! An example of this may be seen in the 2003 exam where students were asked to pick out the word for **sports hall** from the following four:

| SPORTPLATZ | TURNHALLE | GYMNASIUM | LABOR |

The immediate tendency for English speakers would be to choose 'Gymnasium' as that is the word so often shortened to 'gym' in English. However, as you may remember, 'Gymnasium' is a type of second-level school in Germany. The correct word is 'Turnhalle'.

✍️ Now test yourself

(Solutions on p. 93)

1. You are in Germany and you want to go to the **butcher's shop.** Where do you go? **Rewrite** the chosen word.

| MIETSHAUS | GEMÜSELADEN | METZGEREI | KONDITOREI |

2. If you wanted to use the **escalator** in a German store, which sign would you look for? **Rewrite** the chosen word.

| AUFZUG | ROLLTREPPE | ERDGESCHOSS | TREPPE |

3. You are travelling by car in Germany. Which sign indicates a **one-way street**? **Rewrite** the chosen word.

SACKGASSE	KREUZUNG	KREISVERKEHR	EINBAHNSTRASSE

PAST EXAM QUESTION

(Solutions on p. 96)

1. Which of the following expressions would be appropriate to use when wishing someone **to get well soon**? **Rewrite** the chosen word or expression.

HERZLICHEN GLÜCKWUNSCH	GESUNDHEIT	FROHE WEIHNACHTEN	GUTE BESSERUNG

---

2. You are looking for the **history** section in the library. Which heading would you look for? **Rewrite** the chosen word.

GESICHT	GESCHICHTE	ERDKUNDE	GESPRÄCHE

---

3. You are looking for directions to a **travel agency.** What would you ask? **Rewrite** the chosen word.

TOURISTEN-INFORMATION	FAHRSCHULE	REISEBÜRO	FUNDBÜRO

Section B

In this section the task is to match German advertisements to the English words for the items or services being advertised.

There are *seven* advertisements shown and a list of *ten* English terms given. The advertisements are numbered 1 to 7. You must write the *number* of each advertisement opposite the English term for what is being advertised. One number is already filled in as an example, so that leaves *six* advertisements to be matched. Obviously there will be three English words or terms that are not needed. Only six spaces should be used by you. If you write the same number in two spaces you will lose marks.

SAMPLE QUESTION

Write the **number** of the ADVERTISEMENT beside the item, message or service it is advertising. **Beware of extra items!**

Number

1
Braun
Plak Control
Aufsteck
Zahnbürste
sortiert
2 Stück

ÜBER
30%
SPAREN!
8.65
5.95

Number	
	Potato salad
	Pharmacy
	Vacuum cleaner
	Sewing machine
	Toothpaste
	Magazine
7	Sight-seeing from the air
	Gloves
	Toothbrush
	Popcorn

2
Victoria Nähmaschine Trikotstich, Kantenstich, Zick-Zack-Stich, Federstich, Patch-O-matik zum Sticken und Stopfen, CE, TÜV, GS

3
Arbeitshandschuhe Textilrücken und Innenflächen aus Spaltleder

4

Popp
Pellkartoffelsalat
mit Gurken und Zwiebeln
in Salatmayonaise, 1000 g Becher

5

vereinigt mit **Gesundheit** *1. September 2003*

6

Aus dem Hause AEG
PROGRESS
Bodenstaubsauger

PC 4100
1600 Watt, 5-lagiges Feinfilter-System,
2-lagiger Hygienestaubbeutel,
Microfilter

7

Ju52-Rundflug Schwerin – Parchim

Sa. 20. 9. 2003
Flugpreis/Pers. **99,- €**
Flugdauer ca. 20 Min.

Ein besonderer Rundflug – Schwerin liegt in der Nähe Ihres Startflughafens Parchim. Sie sehen das Schweriner Schloss, das 775-jährige Parchim und seine reizvolle Umgebung aus der Luft.

Transhansa Reisen GmbH
23560 Lübeck-Flughafen
Tel. 0451/55 446 · Fax 0451/55 371

Number 7 is already done as an example so the last advertisement may be ignored by you. As this is a test of your understanding of German, you must examine the *text* as well as the *picture* (if there is one) and take care not to be misled.

Some may look quite similar, as is the case here with 'toothpaste' and 'toothbrush'. Remember that the list includes extra items, so there is a strong possibility that one of the two above is needed. Careful examination of the texts will reveal the word 'Zahn*bürste*' in No. 1 beside a picture of a toothbrush.

You may, of course, know some of the key words given in the German texts and this is very reassuring during an exam. For example, No. 3 has the heading 'Arbeitshandschuhe'. You may know that 'Handschuhe' means 'gloves'. However, even if you do not know the word, you can have a fair guess by breaking it down into easy parts: 'Hand' = hand, 'Schuhe' = shoes. Hand shoes? Gloves! 'Arbeit' = work and you know that special gloves are worn for different kinds of work, so No.3 may be written in the space opposite Gloves.

The word 'Apotheken' is among the biggest on the page and may tempt you to match that advertisement with 'pharmacy'. However, ask yourself why a date appears in the advertisement if it is for a pharmacy. And what about 'Illustrierte'? Look through the English again. Is there another possibility? What could be illustrated? A magazine! Would the date appear on a magazine? Yes. So, No.5 is a magazine, and 'pharmacy' is probably an extra item.

'Potato salad' as the first item in English may get your attention first. (There is no recommended order for answering this section.) It will not take you long to find the terms '*Salat*mayonnaise' and 'Pell*kartoffelsalat*' which appear in No.4. You will not be fooled by the *name* 'Popp' on the product.

Only two advertisements (No.2 and No.6) remain unmatched and all of the English terms except 'vacuum cleaner' and 'sewing machine' have been dealt with.

You are more likely to match No.6 first, using the words 'Fein*filter-System*' and 'Microfilter' to identify the vacuum cleaner. If you have a good knowledge of household vocabulary you will already have worked out the word 'Bodenstaubsauger' in the heading.

No.2 contains the word 'maschine' which helps! You may also know 'nähen' (to sew). Otherwise you could guess that 'Stich' and 'Patch' might have something to do with sewing.

The correct answer to the sample question given above is shown here.

Number

4	Potato salad
	Pharmacy
6	Vacuum cleaner
2	Sewing machine
	Toothpaste
5	Magazine
7	Sight-seeing from the air
3	Gloves
1	Toothbrush
	Popcorn

This section may look very easy. It seems that all you have to do is write six figures. However, as you have seen, careful reading of the text is essential. It is very important not to be caught out by the extra items given in English. They are included at higher level to challenge you. Here are some examples of such challenges from past papers. Which would you choose?

Car hire or driving school?

Rail exhibition or
travel agency?

Vacuum cleaning system or
maid service?

If you give this section due care and time, you should be able to get full marks here.

✍ Now test yourself

(Solutions on p. 93)

Write the **number** of the ADVERTISEMENT beside the item, message or service it is advertising. **Beware of extra items!**

Number

	Cruises
	Hair salon
4	Honey
	Pumpkins
	Museum open night
	Candles
	Television set
	Dressmaker
	Festival
	Exhibition

1

Halloween-Kerzen
ca. 18cm

1.99

3er Pack

Lübecker Museumsnacht
27. September 2003

18.00 bis 01.00 Uhr
außerhalb der Altstadt
besondere Öffnungszeiten

Sammelticket - alle Veranstaltungen
Erwachsene   € 7,00
Jugendliche (6-18 Jahre)   € 2,00
und Studierende

Kinder unter 6 Jahren frei

2

DIE HAARSCHNEIDEREI
Andrea Kluschke

Verwöhnen beim Friseur!

✂ Entspannen auf der Waschliege
✂ „Heiße Schere", die besondere Haarpflege

Lübecker Straße 10 · 24306 Plön
Telefon 0 45 22-78 93 80

Öffnungszeiten:
Mo. - Fr. 9.00 - 18.00 Uhr Wir bitten um Ihre Anmeldung

3

4

Biophar Honig aus traditionell konventioneller Imkerei

Linden-Honig cremig, Raps-Honig cremig, Wald-Honig flüssig oder Akazien-Honig flüssig 500g Glas je 3.49 (1 kg = 6.98 €)

Farbfernsehgerät

34cm sichtbare Bildschirmdiagonale, Hyperbandtuner, 100 Programmspeicherplätze, automatischer Sendersuchlauf, OSD´mehrsprachig, Videotext, Sleep-Timer, inkl. Fernbedienung, in Silber

6

Das
A. Paul Weber-Museum

in Ratzeburg, Domhof 5,
zeigt eine neue Sonderaustellung:

RAINER EHRT

Satirische
Zeichnungen und
Künstlerbücher

5. 9. – 30. 11. 2003

geöffnet ist täglich, außer montags,
von 10–13 und 14–17 Uhr

5

7

Kreuzfahrt „Zur Mitternachtssonne"
15-Tage-Kreuzfahrt vom 13.06.–27.06.2004

Kommen Sie an Bord der MS MISTRAL**** und lassen Sie den Alltag hinter sich. Auf kaum einer anderen Reise können sie in der Kürze der Zeit so viele verschiedene Eindrücke sammeln. Dabei ist kein Tag wie der andere, denn Ihr schwimmendes Komfort-Hotel bringt Sie jeden Tag an andere interessante Orte. Gleichzeitig finden Sie an Bord ein Maximum an Erholung und Entspannung. Freuen Sie sich auf ein unvergeßlicles Kreuzfahrterlebnis!

15-Tage-Kreuzfahrt mit MS MISTRAL ****
in der Zweibett-Innenkabine schon ab €

PAST EXAM QUESTION

(Solutions on p. 96)

Write the **number** of the ADVERTISEMENT beside the item or service it is advertising. **Beware of extra items!**

Number

2	Wines
	Riding holidays
	Health food shop
	Guitar lessons
	Sports gym
	Children's shoe shop
	Children's party food
	Second-level school
	TV magazine
	Windows and doors

1

2

3

4

THE **Sound of Silence**...

... **ist Ihnen sicher, wenn Sie sich für HBI Fenster und Haustüren entscheiden:** Ihre schlaflosen Nächte gehören der Vergangenheit an. Denn auch die Schallisolierung unserer Produkte ist nach dem neuesten Stand der Technik entwickelt. Sie haben die Wahl und der Lärm bleibt draußen.

HBI Fenster + Türen

Anzeige ausschneiden und Infomaterial anfordern bei:
HBI-Holz-Bau-Industrie GmbH & Co. KG • Postfach 1162 • 27384 Hemsbünde
Telefon: 04266/933-0 • Telefax: 04266/457 u. 458

5

MALM

Der Naturkostladen auf der Leipziger

Wir freuen uns täglich
von 9.30 bis 18.30 Uhr und Samstags
von 9.00 bis 13.30 Uhr über Ihren Besuch.

Malm Naturkost – Leipziger Straße 18
60487 Frankfurt/Bockenheim
Telefon 069/70 22 27

7

GYMNASIUM FÜR JUGENDLICHE AB 11 JAHREN BEGINN 15. AUGUST

NEUES GYMNASIUM MINERVA

Humanistisches Gymnasium — HG
Math.-Naturwiss. Gymnasium — MNG
Wirtschafts-Gymnasium — WG
Neusprachliches Gymnasium — NSG

Bitte senden Sie mir Ihre Dokumentation

Name . . . .

Adresse . . . .

PLZ/Ort . . . .

Neues Gymnasium Minerva
St. Albanvorstadt 30/32, 4052 Basel
Telefon 281 70 30, Fax 281 70 03

6

Ferienclub POPCORN

Reiterferien vom Feinsten
für junge Leute von 8-16
Prospekt sofort von 04805/227

Section C

In this section longer advertisements in German are presented. You must answer several short questions in English. The answers may need just a word or a phrase. While a text may appear difficult at a first reading, closer examination will show that a good grasp of basic vocabulary is enough to answer successfully.

The following are examples of the type of text and question which appear in section C.

SAMPLE QUESTION

1.

> # 3 Tage Swinging Kopenhagen
> ## Kurzurlaub in Dänemark
> 29.09 – 01.10.2003
> Hotel im Herzen Kopenhagens, geführte Stadtrundfahrt,
> Eintritt Schloss Rosenborg, Eintritt Tivoli
> inkl. Programm Übernachtung/Frühstück
>
> *UNSER PREIS:*
> pro Person ab **€ 299,–**
> Einzelzimmerzuschlag € 81,–
>
> *Infos & Buchung in Ihrem Reisebüro!*

(a) Where in Copenhagen is the hotel situated?

_____

(b) What is included in the price of this holiday? Give **three** details.

_____

_____

_____

(c) What costs an extra €81?

_____

_____

(d) Where is further information available?

_____

At first glance, it looks as if there could not be much information in this short advertisement. Yet, when you read the questions, you realise that there is quite a lot of information given. In fact, by reading the questions *first*, you already gain some understanding of the text.

1. (a) The first question is about the hotel's location. The word 'hotel' appears only once here, 'Hotel im Herzen Kopenhagens', i.e. hotel in the heart of Copenhagen. So your answer is 'in the heart' or 'the middle' or 'the centre'.
    (b) You must now find *three* things included in the price of this holiday. There is so little text here that it is easy to see that the relevant part is from 'geführte Stadtrundfahrt' to 'Frühstück'. 'Frühstück' gives you an easy answer. 'Übernachtung' and 'Stadtrundfahrt' are easy when you break the long words into their shorter parts, e.g. 'Stadt/rund/fahrt'. 'Schloss' is part of the vocabulary you have learned for talking about towns or sightseeing. 'Eintritt' is a word you may not know. Could you make an intelligent guess in the context of a short city holiday? Anyway, you have enough without needing to use it.
        Any three of the following would be acceptable answers:
        *   (Guided) tour of the city
        *   Entrance to (Rosenborg) castle
        *   Entrance to Tivoli
        *   Overnight stay/bed
        *   Breakfast.
    (c) You have to decide what the extra charge of €81 is for. There are only two prices given here. Obviously, the higher price (from €299) refers to the overall cost per person of the three-day holiday. When you break down the word 'Einzelzimmerzuschlag' you will understand 'Einzelzimmer' (single room). The 'zuschlag' must mean the 'extra charge' referred to in the question. The €81 is the single room supplement. Your answer therefore is 'a single room'.
    (d) Where is further information available? The last line tells you: 'Info . . . in Ihrem Reisebüro'. 'Reisebüro' is a travel agency. Answer: In (your) travel agency.

2.

WEITER MOBIL . . .
DAS MUSEUM IM KOFFER

Träger des Nürnberger Kindermuseums ist das Museum im Koffer e.V. Diese mobile Form eines Kindermuseums – das erste seiner Art – ist seit 1980 im Großraum Nürnberg und in ganz Deutschland unterwegs.

Mit dem Transportbus kommen die MitarbeiterInnen des Museums-Teams in die Schule, den Kindergarten, die Bibliothek oder auf das Stadtteilfest. Zu den verschiedenen Themen – insgesamt sind es 22 – bringen sie jeweils eine Vielzahl von Gegenständen mit. Zusätzlich gibt es auch Fotos, Texte, eine Ausstellung und Bücher. Die Kinder können in Gruppen oder einzeln ganze Handlungsabläufe nachvollziehen, und z.B. durch eigenes Arbeiten erfahren, wie es früher war.

(a) Mention **three** details about this museum. **(Paragraph 1)**

_____

_____

_____

(b) List **three** places which may benefit from this museum. **(Paragraph 2)**

_____

_____

_____

(c) Apart from the objects on display, what else can be seen? List **four** items. **(Paragraph 2)**

_____

_____

_____

_____

(d) What can children learn through their own work in this museum? **(Paragraph 2)**

_____

_____

This text may look more difficult because there are full sentences written in a block and you may think it will be harder to find the information. However, this is not the case, as you will see.

2. (a) You are asked for *three* details from Paragraph 1 about the museum. The title and the picture have the words 'im Koffer' (in the suitcase) and the reference is to a mobile museum. It has been 'seit 1980 . . . unterwegs' (on the move since 1980). It has been 'im Großraum Nürnberg und in ganz Deutschland' (in the greater Nürnberg area and in the whole of Germany). It is 'das erste seiner Art' (the first of its kind). The easiest point is in the first line where you can see that this is a 'Kindermuseum' (a museum for children).

Here are the five details given, of which you need only three, so even if you did not know the words 'Großraum' or 'Art', you could still have answered fully:
- Mobile museum/museum on the move
- Children's museum
- First of its kind
- Founded in/on the move since 1980
- Visits the greater Nürnberg area and all of Germany.

(b) You now have to list *three* places which benefit from this museum. This is a very easy question. You will find 'Schule', 'Kindergarten' and 'Bibliothek' which you have known since your first year. For 'Kindergarten', you could write 'nursery school' or you could leave the word in German, since it is a word used in English also. You need only these three, but you may be able to work out the other word 'Stadtteilfest', too. 'Fest' is a festival, 'Stadt' is a town, and 'Teil' is a part, so the whole word refers to a festival in town or a part of town.

Possible answers are:
- School
- Nursery school
- Library
- Town festival.

(c) Here you are asked for *four* items to be seen apart from the objects in the museum. You see the word 'auch' (also) followed by a list of four things. Again, three of the four are very easy. 'Fotos', 'Texte' and 'Bücher' will be no problem for you. 'Ausstellung' means 'exhibition' or 'display'.

- Photos
- Texts
- An exhibition/display
- Books

(d) The last task is to find out what children can learn through their own work in this museum. You see that 'Die *Kinder* können . . . durch eigenes *Arbeiten* erfahren, wie es früher war'. So what they learn must be 'wie es früher war', i.e. 'how it was earlier' or 'how it used to be' or 'what life was like in the past'. It is, after all, a museum.

☞ *Now test yourself*

(Solutions on p. 93)

Read through the advertisement and answer the questions **in English.**

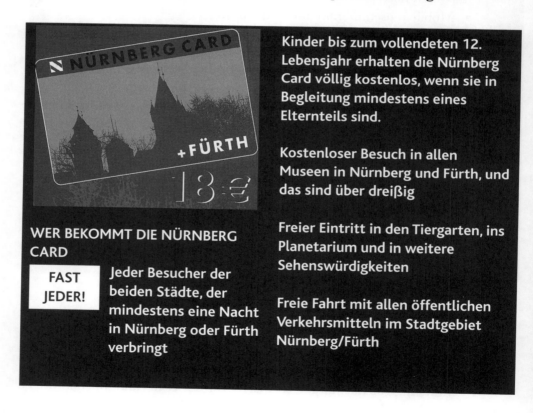

WER BEKOMMT DIE NÜRNBERG CARD

FAST JEDER!

Jeder Besucher der beiden Städte, der mindestens eine Nacht in Nürnberg oder Fürth verbringt

Kinder bis zum vollendeten 12. Lebensjahr erhalten die Nürnberg Card völlig kostenlos, wenn sie in Begleitung mindestens eines Elternteils sind.

Kostenloser Besuch in allen Museen in Nürnberg und Fürth, und das sind über dreißig

Freier Eintritt in den Tiergarten, ins Planetarium und in weitere Sehenswürdigkeiten

Freie Fahrt mit allen öffentlichen Verkehrsmitteln im Stadtgebiet Nürnberg/Fürth

Holen Sie sich als Geschenk zwei Postkarten und ein Fotoplakat in der Tourist Information in Nürnberg ab

10 bis 20 Prozent Nachlass in mehreren Theatern in beiden Städten, im Paradies Revue-Theater und im IMAX-Kino in Nürnberg.

10 bis 20 Prozent Ermäßigung in vielen Geschäften in Nürnberg und Fürth sowie in den drei Tourist Informationen

10 bis 20 Prozent Ermäßigung bei den Stadtführungen und Stadtrundfahrten in beiden Städten

EIN BEISPIEL:
FÜR ZWEI ERWACHSENE UND EIN KIND

(inkl. zwei Tage freier Fahrt mit den öffentlichen Verkehrsmitteln)

1. Tag:	Vormittags: Nachmittags: Abends:	Shopping in der Altstadt Spielzeugmuseum Besuch Gostner Hoftheater (ohne Kinder)
2. Tag:	Vormittags: Nachmittags:	Tiergarten DB Museum und Museum für Kommunikation

2 x Nürnberg Card für Erwachsene:	36,– €
1 x Nürnberg Card für Kinder	0,– €
Gesamt	36,– €
Ersparnis mindestens	7,10 €

1. Who is entitled to get a Nürnberg card? Give details.

_____

_____

2. Under what **two** conditions can a child get a free Nürnberg card?

_____

_____

3. List **four** things which are free for holders of a Nürnberg card.

_____

_____

_____

_____

4. Give **three** examples of where card holders are offered a reduction of 10 to 20 per cent.

_____

_____

_____

5. The advertisement includes an example of the activities possible for two adults and one child under this scheme. List **four** things that they can all do together.

_____

_____

_____

_____

PAST EXAM QUESTION

(Solutions on p. 96)

Read through the advertisements, and answer the questions **in English**:

1.

MAYO HORSEDRAWN CARAVAN HOLIDAYS

Belcarra, Castlebar,
Co. Mayo
Tel/Fax 00 353 94 32054

Entdecken Sie Westirland! Mit einem Pferdewagen und ruhigem Pferd ist es möglich! Sie können wandern, mit dem Rad fahren und Land und Leute kennenlernen.

Abends können Sie irische Volksmusik in den freundlichen Kneipen hören und in gastfreundlichen Pensionen übernachten. Für einen besonders umweltfreundlichen Urlaub rufen Sie uns einfach an.

(a) Mention **three** details listed in the advertisement which make holidaying in a horsedrawn caravan attractive.

_____

_____

_____

(b) What can people do in the evenings?

_____

_____

(c) Where can one stay overnight?

_____

2.

GESUCHT

Ältere Dame in Einfamilienhaus auf dem Lande sucht

liebevolle Haushaltshilfe.

Suchen Sie eine Arbeit für 4 Tage und Nächte in der Woche?
Möchten Sie ein eigenes Zimmer mit Bad?
Haben Sie ein eigenes Auto?
Dann schreiben Sie an
Chiffre K412952 an PUBLICITAS,
Postfach, 4010 Basel.

(a) An elderly lady is looking for a housekeeper. Where does she live?

_____

_____

(b) What are the times of work?

_____

(c) What should the applicant own?

_____

Section D

There are three questions in this section. In each question you are asked to identify and rewrite the *one* correct sentence among four. The sentences are part of everyday school language used by teachers and pupils. If you follow these few guidelines, you will have no problem. You already know your basic school vocabulary, so you just need to study the specific forms used. Generally, the *pronoun* (du, ihr, Sie) will indicate the person/s being spoken to. Look at the following examples.

'Hast *du* deine Hausaufgaben gemacht?' (Did you do your homework?) This could be a teacher talking to a pupil *or* a pupil talking to a pupil.

'Habt *ihr* Fragen?' (Have you any questions?). This is most likely a teacher talking to more than one pupil or to the class.

'Können *Sie* das bitte erklären?' (Can you explain that please?) This is a pupil talking to a teacher.

Of course you will also come across sentences without these pronouns. Examples:

Soll ich den Kassettenrekorder holen?	Should I get the cassette recorder?
Darf ich auf die Toilette gehen?	May I go to the toilet?
Schreiben wir heute eine Arbeit?	Are we doing a test today?
Wer fehlt heute?	Who is missing today?
Morgen ist schulfrei.	There is no school tomorrow.
Heute ist die Schule um 12 Uhr aus.	School is over at 12 o'clock today.

When somebody is giving *an order*, i.e. telling somebody to do something, *the pronoun is dropped*. However, it is still easy to identify the correct sentence:

1. *When talking to a pupil:*

*   **du machst** you do > **Mach!** Do.
    Example: **Mach deine Hausaufgaben!** Do your homework.
    Note the use of the exclamation mark (!) when giving an order in German.

*   **du gibst** you give > **Gib!** Give.
    Example: **Gib mir bitte die Kreide!** Give me the chalk, please.

*   **du setzt dich** you sit down > **Setz dich!** Sit down.

*   **du liest** you read > **Lies!** Read.
    Example: **Lies Seite 21!** Read Page 21.

*   Sometimes 'e' is added to the verb, e.g.
    du wartest you wait > **Warte!** Wait.

*   Note: 'sein' to be
    du bist you are > **Sei!** Be.
    Example: **Sei** still! Be quiet.

2. *When talking to more than one person, i.e. pupils/class:*

The verb form ends in 't' or 'et' except for the verb 'sein'.
*   **ihr macht** you do > **Macht!** Do.
    Example: **Macht die Übung auf Seite 14!** Do the exercise on page 14.

*   **ihr nehmt** you take > **Nehmt!** Take.
    Example: **Nehmt eure Hefte heraus!** Take out your copies.

*   **ihr setzt euch** you sit down >**Setzt euch!** Sit down.

*   **ihr wartet** you wait > **Wartet!** Wait.

*   Note: 'sein' to be
    ihr seid you are > **Seid!** Be.
    Example: **Seid bitte ruhig!** Be quiet, please.

Try these!

In which one of the following is the teacher telling *more* than one pupil to bring the chairs into the garden?
(a) 'Bringt die Stühle in den Garten!'
(b) 'Bring die Stühle in den Garten!'

In which one is the teacher telling *one* pupil to listen?
(a) 'Hört bitte zu!'
(b) 'Hör bitte zu!'

3. *When a pupil is talking to a teacher:*

•   **Sie schreiben** You write > **Schreiben Sie!** Write.
    Example: **Schreiben Sie das bitte an die Tafel!** Please write that on the board.

•   **Sie buchstabieren** You spell > **Buchstabieren Sie!** Spell.
    Example: **Bitte buchstabieren Sie das Wort!** Please spell the word.

Here are examples of some *separable verbs* which occur in classroom vocabulary:

aufmachen	to open
Macht die Bücher auf!	Open the books.
zumachen	to close
Macht die Bücher zu!	Close the books.
aufpassen	to pay attention
Pass bitte auf!	Please pay attention.
anfangen	to start
Fangt jetzt an zu schreiben!	Start writing now.
einsammeln	to collect
Sammle die Hefte ein!	Collect the copies.
aufhören	to stop
Hör auf zu reden!	Stop talking.
aufschreiben	to write down
Schreibt das auf!	Write/take that down.
abschreiben	to copy
Schreib nicht ab!	Don't copy!

In each of the following questions, indicate your answer by **writing the appropriate sentence on the line provided**.

1. The teacher wants the class to open page 12 of their books. What does he/she say?
   (a) Lest Seite 12!
   (b) Schlag Seite 12 auf!
   (c) Macht die Übung auf Seite 12!
   (d) Schlagt Seite 12 auf!

   _____

The first one is 'Lest' (Read) and the third one is 'Macht' (Do) 'die Übung' (the exercise). Obviously neither of these is suitable. So, you are left with a choice of two, which at first glance look quite similar. However, if you have studied the guidelines given above, you will see that in (d) the verb ends in 't', the form used to address *more* than one pupil/the class. The correct answer is therefore (d): 'Schlagt Seite 12 auf!'

2. You want to ask your teacher if he/she could repeat something. What do you say?
   (a) Wie schreibt man das, bitte?
   (b) Kannst du das wieder vorlesen?
   (c) Können Sie das bitte wiederholen?
   (d) Sprechen Sie bitte langsamer!

   _____

The second one can be ruled out straightaway because it has the pronoun 'du' and you know that when speaking to a teacher you use the pronoun 'Sie'. Also it has the verb 'vorlesen': 'lesen' (to read), 'vorlesen' (to read out). In the first one you are asking how something is written: 'Wie schreibt man das?'. The last one has 'Sprechen' (speak) and 'langsamer' (more slowly). If you don't know 'langsamer', note the absence of the question mark and remember 'You want to *ask* your teacher if . . .'.

   The correct answer is (c): 'Können Sie das bitte wiederholen?'. Even if you don't know the whole word 'wiederholen', you know 'wieder' (again) and you can see that it would have been possible to identify the correct answer.

(Solutions on p. 93)

In each of the following three questions, indicate your answer by **writing the appropriate sentence on the line provided**.

1. On behalf of your class, you want to ask your teacher if you are getting your tests back today. What do you say?
    (a) Kriegen wir die Arbeiten heute wieder?
    (b) Wir haben die Arbeit sehr schwer gefunden.
    (c) Schreiben wir heute wieder eine Arbeit?
    (d) Bekommen wir heute die Zeugnisse?

    _____

2. The teacher tells you to look something up in the dictionary. What does he/she say?
    (a) Nehmt eure Wörterbücher heraus!
    (b) Du findest das in deinem Vokabelheft.
    (c) Schau das im Wörterbuch nach!
    (d) Hol das Wörterbuch, bitte!

    _____

3. Your teacher lets you know that there will be no German class tomorrow. What does he/she say?
    (a) Morgen bleibt ihr nach der Deutschstunde im Klassenzimmer.
    (b) Morgen ist unsere deutsche Assistentin nicht da.
    (c) Ihr braucht morgen keine Bücher in der Deutschstunde.
    (d) Morgen fällt die Deutschstunde aus.

    _____

PAST EXAM QUESTION

(Solutions on p. 96)

In the case of each of the following three questions, indicate your answer by **writing the appropriate sentence on the line provided**.

1. You want to ask your teacher if **you** may open the window. What do you say?
   (a) Mach das Fenster auf!
   (b) Soll ich das Fenster zumachen?
   (c) Darf ich das Fenster aufmachen?
   (d) Können Sie das Fenster aufmachen?

   _____

2. Your teacher tells the class to write down the homework. What does he/she say?
   (a) Schreib bitte die Hausaufgaben ab!
   (b) Schreibt bitte die Hausaufgaben auf!
   (c) Morgen schreibt ihr eine Klassenarbeit!
   (d) Zeigt mir gleich eure Hausaufgaben!

   _____

3. You can't concentrate on what is being said in class because your classmate keeps talking! How would you ask/tell him/her to be quiet?
   (a) Seid bitte endlich mal still!
   (b) Hören Sie endlich mal zu!
   (c) Rede nicht so leise!
   (d) Sei bitte ruhig!

   _____

Section E

In this section there are four notices or advertisements in German. The information required must be filled into a grid in English.

SAMPLE QUESTION

Read through the following notices in which young people are seeking penpals. Fill in the information required, **in English**, in the spaces provided. The information from Box (1) has been filled in as an example.

1

Ich heiße Daniel und komme aus Hamburg. Ich suche einen Brieffreund aus Frankreich. Ich lerne sehr gern Französisch. Ich sehe gern fern, spiele Schach und ich gehe gern ins Kino. Ich spiele Geige. Ich mag klassische Musik, aber Discomusik finde ich langweilig.

2

Ich heiße Rebekka, bin 12 Jahre alt und komme aus Wien. Ich suche eine Brieffreundin aus England oder Irland. Ich möchte meine Englischkenntnisse verbessern. Ich sehe gern fern, lese gern und höre gern Musik. Ich kann Sport überhaupt nicht leiden. Ich spiele kein Instrument.

3

Ich heiße Christian, bin 14 Jahre alt und komme aus Köln. Ich mag Sport, besonders Wassersport, Kanufahren und Tauchen. Ich gehe gern mit meinem Hund spazieren. Ich finde deutsche Popmusik blöd. Ich suche Brieffreunde aus aller Welt, denn ich reise sehr gern. Ich spiele Klavier.

4

Ich heiße Melanie und bin 15 Jahre alt. Ich komme aus Stuttgart und suche einen Brieffreund oder eine Brieffreundin aus Italien. Ich war letztes Jahr mit meinen Eltern in Rom und fand den Ort super. Ich spiele Flöte. Ich schwimme gern, fahre gern Rad und gehe gern einkaufen. Hobbys, die ich nicht mag, sind Nähen und Basteln.

	Seeks penpal/s from	Reason for choice	Hobbies	Musical instrument played	One dislike
1	France	Likes learning French	Television Chess Cinema	Violin	Disco music
2					
3					
4					

1. It is important to study the example and to note the information given under each heading. This will help you with your own answers. Sometimes students lose marks here, not through lack of knowledge, but through lack of care. For instance, the first heading refers to the *penpal's* home place, not to the home of the person seeking a penpal.

   It is worth noting also that in this section most of the information given in German will be needed in your answers. There is very little irrelevant material.

2. Rebekka wants a penpal from *England or Ireland*. Reason? She would like *to improve her English*: 'Englischkenntnisse verbessern'. Her hobbies are *watching television, reading* and *listening to music*. She plays 'kein Instrument', which means that you should write *None* under the heading 'Musical instrument played'. Do not leave a blank space. Rebekka says, 'Ich kann Sport überhaupt nicht leiden' which means that she absolutely cannot bear/stand *sport*. Even without understanding 'leiden', you have 'nicht' to indicate a negative.

3. You will find all the information you need, although it is not given in the same order as before. There is no country mentioned, but you will see that Christian wants penpals 'aus aller Welt' (*from all over the world*). Why? Because he *loves travelling*: 'ich reise sehr gern'. He enjoys *sport*, especially *water sports* such as *canoeing* and *diving* ('Tauchen'). He also likes *going for a walk with his dog*. He plays the *piano* ('Klavier'). He says he finds *German pop music* 'blöd' (stupid).

4. Melanie wants a penpal from *Italy*. Why? She *visited Rome* last year with her parents and *loved it* ('fand den Ort super'). She enjoys *swimming, cycling* and *shopping* ('gehe gern einkaufen'). She dislikes *sewing* ('Nähen') and craftwork ('Basteln'). She plays the *flute* ('Flöte').

✍ Now test yourself

(Solutions on p. 94)

Read through the following advertisements for hotels. Then fill in the information required, **in English,** in the spaces provided. The required information from Box (1) has been filled in as an example.

1
> **Hotel Valentin.** Am Stadtrand gelegen. Gute Busverbindung in die Stadt. 20 Einzelzimmer und 40 Doppelzimmer mit Bad/Dusche. Schöner Blick auf das Schloss. Seniorenermäßigung. Kegelbahn und gute Einkaufsmöglichkeiten in der Nähe.

2
> **Hotel Seeblick.** Nur 5 Minuten zu Fuß zum Strand. Zimmer mit Kinderbetten. Großer Balkon, Tiefgarage und Hallenbad. Ideal zum Surfen, Schwimmen und Segeln. Kinder- und hunde-freundlich. Herrlicher Blick auf die See und den Strand.

3
> **Hotel Hirsch.** Mitten im Schwarzwald. In ruhiger Lage. 100 Betten. Zimmersafe. Geheiztes Hallenbad. Möglichkeit zum Wandern im herrlichen Wald. Schöne Ausflüge in der Umgebung. Frühstücksbüffet auf der Terrasse. Hunde sind willkommen.

4
> **Hotel am See.** Direkt am See gelegen. Alle Zimmer mit Bad/Dusche. Fitnessraum, Solarium, Parkplatz. Tolle Wassersport-möglichkeiten in der Nähe und schöne Radwege für begeisterte Radfahrer. Kinderfreundlich. Tiere nicht erlaubt.

	Situation	Facilities	Activities	Two other details
1	Just outside town	20 single rooms 40 double rooms with shower/bath	Shopping Bowling	View of castle Good bus connection to town Reduction for senior citizens
2				
3				
4				

PAST EXAM QUESTION
(Solutions on p. 97)

Read through the following notices about suggested activities from a local newspaper. Then fill in the information required, **in English**, in the spaces provided. The required information from Box (1) has been filled in as an example.

KULTURNOTIZEN

1

Führung in Museum
Aquarien stehen bei vielen Familien zu Hause. Wer mehr über Fische wissen möchte, sollte ein Angebot des Museums für Naturkunde in der Rosenallee nutzen. Es lädt am Sonntag ab 15 Uhr zu einer **Führung durch die Fischsammlung** ein. Ein Experte gibt Tipps und Ratschläge für Aquarienfreunde.

2

Karneval
Die tollen Tage sind da! Wer Spaß am Fasching hat, sollte am Sonntag zum Checkpoint an der Leipziger Straße gehen. Ab 11 Uhr wird zum „**Karneval für Kinder"** eingeladen. Kinder können Masken basteln und Pfannkuchen essen. Für die Erwachsenen gibt es ein Frühstück.

3

Tanzparty
Für alle Tanz- und Musikfans gibt es am Sonnabend eine **Tanzparty mit Weltmusik**. Von 20 bis 24 Uhr sind Sie in den Spiegelsaal an der Karlstraße 7 eingeladen. Der Eintritt kostet fünf Mark. Das Geld wird an ein Jugendprojekt in Ruanda geschickt.

4

Jazz
Jazz für Kinder gibt es am Freitag um 17 Uhr im Opernhaus an der Behrstraße 55. Kinder ab 10 Jahre sind herzlich willkommen. Eintritt frei. Kinder können verschiedene Instrumente spielen.

	Activity	For whom?	When (day, time)?	Two further details about activity
1	Guided tour in museum	Anyone who would like to know more about fish	Sunday, from 3 p.m.	Offered by Natural History Museum Tour of fish collection Tips and advice from expert
2				
3				
4				

Section F

In this section you must answer questions in English on a longer German piece in the style of a newspaper or magazine article. The text is more demanding than in the earlier sections, but remember that you will not need to understand every word. You are not asked to translate the article, but only to answer some questions. In fact, if you read the questions first, you will have a good idea of the content of the German text.

SAMPLE QUESTION

Read through this article and answer the questions which follow **in English**.

VERLORENE KINDHEIT

Ralf, 14 Jahre: „Ich arbeite nebenher als Zeitungsausträger, zwei bis dreieinhalb Stunden mittwochs. Es macht mir Spaß, und so kann ich mir Geld für Urlaub und Klassenfahrt sparen."

Zeitungen austragen und Babysitten dürften wohl die häufigsten Schülerjobs in Deutschland sein, daneben auch Verkaufs-, Lager- und Hilfsarbeitertätigkeiten. Das Geld dient in fast allen Fällen zur Taschengeld-aufbesserung: CDs, Computerspiele, Disco, Klassenfahrt und Urlaub, Klamotten, Sportarten u.a. In fast allen Fällen gehen die Schülerinnen und Schüler freiwillig solchen Jobs nach; einige bedauern es, keine passende Beschäftigung zu finden.

Ist das so in Ordnung? Wo kann man die Grenze ziehen zwischen „normaler" Kinderarbeit und „schädlicher" Kinderarbeit? Was unterscheidet Kinderarbeit in Deutschland von Kinderarbeit in Brasilien, Kolumbien oder Indien?

In Ländern, wo die Arbeit der Eltern für das Essen und die Kleidung der Familie nicht ausreicht, müssen die Kinder oft arbeiten. Aber man muss fragen, wann Arbeit anfängt, Kinder körperlich oder seelisch zu schädigen.

Shilpi ist eine 14jährige Textilarbeiterin aus Milpur. Sie fand als Hilfskraft in einer Bekleidungsfabrik Arbeit und faltet dort Hemden. Sie verdient 400 Taka im Monat (1 Taka = 8 Pfennige). Sie sagt, dass sie sehr gerne zur Schule gehen würde, aber dass sie sich zuerst um ihren Lebensunterhalt kümmern muss. „Ich muss für mich selbst sorgen. Wie kann ich zur Schule gehen?" Auf die Frage nach ihren Zukunftsplänen sagt sie, dass sie gerne Lehrerin werden möchte. Früher unterrichtete sie manchmal ihren Bruder. „Ich habe ihm das Lesen beigebracht", sagt sie.

---

1. (a) Ralf works on Wednesdays. **What** is his part-time job and **how long** does he work?
   (b) What does he do with his earnings? **(Paragraph 1)**

   (a) Part-time job _____

       How long? _____

   (b) _____

2. (a) Why do young people in Germany have part-time jobs? Give details.
   (b) What comment is made about most of these young people?
                                                        (Paragraph 2)

   (a) _____

       _____

       _____

   (b) _____

       _____

       _____

3. What does the writer describe as 'normal' in Germany and 'harmful' in some
   other parts of the world?   **(Paragraph 3)**

   _____

4. Why are children often obliged to work?   **(Paragraph 4)**

   _____

   _____

5. (a) **Where** does Shilpi work and **what** does she do there?
   (b) **What** would Shilpi like to be in the future and **why** might that be a good
       choice?   **(Paragraph 5)**

   (a) Where? _____

       What? _____

   (b) What? _____

       Why? _____

Having read the questions, you see that the article is about young people working. Now try to work out the meaning of the title 'Verlorene Kindheit'. 'Kind' is child, 'Kindheit' is childhood. What does 'ich habe mein Buch *verloren*' mean? If you know that 'verloren' means lost, you can translate the title as 'Lost Childhood'. This may not make sense to you, but its relevance will become clear when you have finished work on the article. (It is important not to ignore the heading on an article as it is usually helpful. If you don't understand it, don't panic. The text will be easy enough to deal with because you are given directions as to which sections to use for your answers.)

1. In this article, the first paragraph contains a lot of information in a few lines. You must find out *what* Ralf does as a part-time job and *how long* he works. You are also asked what he does with his earnings.
    (a) You notice that Ralf is 14 years old. He says, 'Ich arbeite nebenher als Zeitungsausträger.' You know from your basic vocabulary that 'Zeitung' means 'newspaper'. The second part of the word 'austräger' is more difficult. What could a 14-year-old be doing with a newspaper as a *part-time job*? Editing? Reporting? Reading? Hardly likely. What does 'aus' mean here? Out. So, something to do with giving *out*. Delivering/ distributing? Much more likely. So your answer is that he delivers/ distributes newspapers or that he is a newspaper delivery boy.
       You are told that Ralf works on Wednesdays. You can see 'zwei bis dreieinhalb Stunden mittwochs' at the end of the first sentence. It is not hard to work out 'two to three and a half hours'.
    (b) You find out what he does with his earnings from the words 'Geld' (money) and 'sparen' (to save). What is he saving for? 'Urlaub und Klassenfahrt'. He saves for 'a holiday/holidays and a class/school trip'.

2. (a) The first sentence of Paragraph 2 deals with other common part-time jobs in Germany. You are asked *why* young people have these jobs. The answer is in the second sentence, which contains the word 'Taschengeld-aufbesserung'. This may look scary, but it has 'Taschengeld' and 'besser' among its parts. Better pocket money? The money earned in a part-time job improves their pocket money. You were asked for *details*. A full answer would include: extra money on top of/improvement on pocket money for
       • CDs   • Holiday
       • Computer games   • Clothes
       • Disco   • Sport.
       • Class/school trip

(b) What comment is made about most of these young workers? 'In *fast allen* Fällen gehen die Schülerinnen und Schüler *freiwillig* solchen Jobs nach'. 'In fast allen Fällen' (in nearly all cases); 'freiwillig' . . . 'free will'? The answer is that 'they work of their own free will/willingly'. Further study of the article will confirm your answer here.

3. You are asked what the writer describes as normal in Germany but harmful in some other parts of the world. The last sentence in Paragraph 3 contrasts 'Kinderarbeit' in Germany with that in Brazil, Colombia or India. Although you may not know the word 'schädlicher', you can see that it is being contrasted with 'normaler', again referring to 'Kinderarbeit'. It is not hard to work out the meaning of 'Kinderarbeit'. The answer is 'child labour' or 'children's work'.

4. You must find in Paragraph 4 the reason why children are often obliged to work. The first sentence contains the necessary information: 'die Arbeit der Eltern' (the parents' work); 'für das Essen und die Kleidung der Familie' (for the food and clothing of the family); 'nicht' is clearly a negative. You should have enough to go on here to answer that the reason the children must often work ('müssen die Kinder oft arbeiten') is that the parents' work is not sufficient ('nicht ausreicht') to feed and clothe the family.

5. (a) You are asked where Shilpi works and what she does there. She is described as a 14-year-old 'Textilarbeiterin aus Milpur' (a textile worker from Milpur). This does not tell *where* she works, but it does give a possible answer to *what* she does. The next sentence states that she found work 'in einer Bekleidungsfabrik' (a clothing factory), which makes sense, as she is a textile worker, and that she 'faltet dort Hemden' (she folds shirts there). You will recognise 'Hemden' and perhaps you could make an intelligent guess at 'faltet'. However, you would get marks for answering that she is a textile worker.
Answers: Where? In a clothing factory
What? Textile worker/She folds shirts.
(b) You are asked *what* Shilpi would like to be in the future. You should easily find 'dass sie gerne Lehrerin werden möchte' in answer to a question about her future plans ('Frage nach ihren Zukunftsplänen'). She would like to be a teacher.
Why might it be a good choice? 'Früher unterrichtete sie manchmal ihren Bruder.' (She used to teach her brother sometimes.) She says, 'Ich habe ihm das Lesen beigebracht'. (I taught him reading.) She must be good!

Read through this article and answer the questions which follow **in English**.

FRÖHLICHE WEIHNACHTEN ÜBERALL?

Weihnachten – Tannenbaum, Lebkuchen, Kerzenlicht, Spielzeuge, Weihnachtslieder, Geschenke und Liebe. In Deutschland, so wie in den meisten Ländern der Welt, ist Weihnachten eine magische Zeit für Kinder. Sie freuen sich auf das große Fest. Neugierig und aufgeregt an den Tagen vor Weihnachten, warten sie auf lang begehrte Geschenke und in den meisten Fällen werden sie am 24. Dezember nicht enttäuscht.

Doch nicht alle Kinder haben es so gut. Für viele Kinder ist Weihnachten eine traurige Zeit. Familien sind zerstritten, die Eltern sind geschieden oder arbeitslos und die Wünsche der Kinder bleiben unerfüllt. So ist es für Eva, Dominik und Mathias. „Fröhliche Weihnachten" ist für sie nur ein Traum.

Eva ist vierzehn und bei ihr zu Hause gibt es nur Stress und finanzielle Probleme. „Ich habe nette Freunde, aber manchmal fühle ich mich trotzdem isoliert. Sie tragen so schicke Klamotten, gehen auf Konzerte und kaufen regelmäßig teure CDs. Für solche Sachen habe ich kein Geld. Mein größter Wunsch für Weihnachten ist ein cooles Handy. Fast alle Schüler in meiner Klasse haben eins. Wenn du keins hast, gehörst du nicht zur Clique."

Dominik ist dreizehn. Er kommt aus Ungarn und wohnt seit zwei Jahren in Deutschland. Seine Familie war sehr arm und suchte ein besseres Leben in Deutschland. Am Anfang hatte er Schwierigkeiten in der Schule, weil er nicht viel Deutsch konnte. Dann hat sein Vater seine Arbeitsstelle verloren. Die Familie lebt jetzt vom Arbeitslosengeld. „Wenn die Freunde von Weihnachten reden, werde ich nur traurig. Die Computerspiele und die neuesten CDs sind für mich nur ein Traum. Ich liebe Musik und der größte Wunsch auf dem Wunschzettel für das Christkind ist ein tragbarer CD-Spieler."

Mathias ist elf Jahre alt und Einzelkind. Seine Eltern sind geschieden und er wohnt bei seiner Mutter. Er freut sich nicht auf Weihnachten und hat nur einen Wunsch: „Ich vermisse meinen Vater. Mein großer Wunsch ist, dass er Weihnachten mal wieder bei uns ist. Dafür würde ich gerne auf Geschenke verzichten."

1. List **four** pleasant things associated with Christmas which are mentioned in the text.

   (Paragraph 1)

   _____

   _____

2. Why is Christmas sad for many children? Give **two** reasons.

   (Paragraph 2)

   _____

   _____

3. (a) Why does Eva sometimes feel isolated from her friends? Give details.
   (b) Why would she like a mobile phone for Christmas?   **(Paragraph 3)**

   (a) _____

   _____

   _____

   (b) _____

   _____

4. (a) What was life like for Dominik and his family when they moved to Germany? Give details.
   (b) **What** would Dominik like for Christmas and **from whom** would he hope to get one?

   (Paragraph 4)

   (a) _____

   _____

   _____

   (b) _____

   _____

5. What would Mathias like for Christmas?   **(Paragraph 5)**

   _____

(Solutions on p. 98)

Read through this article and answer the questions below **in English**.

HILFE IM AUSLAND UND BEI KATASTROPHEN

Deutsches Rotes Kreuz

Ich heiße Nicole, bin siebenund-zwanzig Jahre alt und wohne in der Nähe von Mainz. Ich bin Krankenschwester und bin auch Mitglied beim Roten Kreuz.

Während des Kosovo Krieges habe ich in einem Flüchtlingscamp gearbeitet. Dort habe ich ein Krankenhaus mit aufgebaut, den Ärzten geholfen und im Operationssaal gearbeitet. Ich habe gekocht und Essen, Kleidung und Spielzeug ausgegeben.

Das Rote Kreuz hilft allen Menschen, im Kosovo also den Serben und den Albanern. Dreizehn Wochen war ich im Kosovo. Vorher war ich schon viermal in Krisengebieten: in Russland, Vietnam und zweimal in Afrika. Frauen, kleine Kinder und alte Leute sind in der Not immer am schlimmsten dran. Sie müssen vor den Soldaten fliehen und haben oft großen Hunger.

Nahrung und Kleidung sind wichtig, um ein normales Leben zu führen. Darum hilft das Rote Kreuz mit sauberem Wasser, Essen, aber auch mit Kleidung wie Thermo-Unterwäsche, warmen Socken, Schuhen, Jacken und Pullovern. Es sammelt auch Bettdecken und für die Babys Windeln, Puder und Seife.

Haben Sie Interesse zu helfen? Dies ist nur ein Beispiel unserer Arbeit. Auch Sie können uns helfen: Mit Geld oder auch, indem Sie ein halbes Jahr mit uns im Inland oder im Ausland arbeiten. Aktiv sind wir zum Beispiel auch im Jugendrotkreuz, im Rettungsdienst und bei der Hilfe für alte oder arme Menschen. Auch Sie können aktiv werden!

Rufen Sie uns an. 0800–4141410 Geldspenden bitte auf das Konto 100 100 50 bei der Deutschen Bank.

---

1. Give **three** details about the Red Cross volunteer, Nicole. **(Paragraph 1)**

   _____

   _____

2. Nicole worked in a refugee camp in Kosovo. Mention **four** jobs she did there.
   (Paragraph 2)

   _____

   _____

3. (a) How long did Nicole spend working in Kosovo?
   (b) Who suffers most in times of catastrophe or war, according to Nicole?
   (Paragraph 3)

   (a) _____

   (b) _____

4. Mention **five** items the Red Cross supplies to people in need. **(Paragraph 4)**

   _____

   _____

5. Mention **three** ways of helping the work of the Red Cross. **(Paragraph 5)**

   _____

   _____

   _____

Section G

In this section, as in Section F, the task is to answer questions in English on a longer German passage. Here the style is literary. The piece is usually a story written in the past tense. You should be familiar with the Perfect Tense, e.g. 'ich habe gemacht'/'ich bin gegangen', in your oral and written work, but it is important also to *recognise* common verbs in the Imperfect Tense, e.g. 'ich machte'/'ich ging'. This tense is frequently used in the type of literary extract which appears in Section G.

   If you read the questions first, you will have some initial idea of the content of the passage. Each question indicates the paragraph or lines in which the answer is to be found. It is also helpful to remember that the questions are given in the order in which the information appears in the text. You may expect the first question to refer to the first part of the text and the last question to refer to near the end of the text.

SAMPLE QUESTION

Answer **in English** the questions which follow the passage.

SCHULJAHR ZU ENDE

Der Sommer kam, und plötzlich war das Schuljahr zu Ende. Am letzten Schultag gab es eine Feier und viel Gesang und Gejodel. Am Ende des Nachmittags bekam jedes Kind eine Wurst und ein Stück Brot, und sie gingen lachend heim durchs Dorf und machten Pläne für den kommenden Tag. Annas Sommerferien hatten begonnen.

Max hatte erst ein paar Tage später frei. In der höheren Schule in Zürich endete das   **5** Schuljahr nicht mit Jodeln und Wurst, sondern mit Zeugnissen.

Max brachte die üblichen Bemerkungen nach Hause: „Strengt sich nicht genug an" und „Zeigt kein Interesse", und er und Anna saßen wie auch sonst bei einem freudlosen Mittagessen, während Papa und Mama das Zeugnis lasen. Mama war besonders enttäuscht. Sie hatte sich daran gewöhnt, dass Max „sich nicht anstrengte" und „kein   **10** Interesse zeigte", solange sie in Deutschland waren, aber aus irgendeinem Grund hatte sie gehofft, es würde in der Schweiz anders sein, denn Max war begabt, er arbeitete nur nicht. Aber der einzige Unterschied war der, dass Max in Deutschland die Arbeit vernachlässigt hatte, um Fußball zu spielen, in der Schweiz hatte er sie vernachlässigt, um zu angeln.   **15**

Wenn Max nicht fischte, schwammen er und Anna und die drei Zwirn-Kinder im See oder spielten miteinander oder gingen in den Wald. Max verstand sich gut mit Franz und Anna hatte Vreneli ganz gern. Trudi war erst sechs, aber sie lief immer hinterher, ganz gleich, was die anderen taten.

Dann kamen eines Morgens Max und Anna nach unten und sahen, dass die Zwirn-   **20** Kinder mit einem Jungen und einem Mädchen spielten, die sie nie zuvor gesehen hatten. Es waren Deutsche, ungefähr in ihrem Alter, und sie verbrachten die Ferien mit ihren Eltern im Gasthaus.

„Aus welchem Teil Deutschlands kommt ihr?", fragte Max.

„München", sagte der Junge.   **25**

„Wir haben früher in Berlin gewohnt", sagte Anna.

„Mensch", sagte der Junge, „Berlin muss prima sein."

Sie spielten alle zusammen Fangen. Es hatte früher nie viel Spaß gemacht, weil sie nur zu viert waren – (Trudi zählte nicht, weil sie nicht schnell genug laufen konnte und immer schrie, wenn jemand sie fing). Aber die deutschen Kinder waren beide sehr flink* auf den   **30** Beinen, und zum ersten Mal war das Spiel wirklich aufregend.

* **flink** = nimble, quick

---

1. What happened on the last day of Anna's school year? Give **four** details.
   (Lines 1–4)

   _____

   _____

   _____

2. Mention **two** ways in which things were different for Max in the higher school in Zürich. **(Lines 5–6)**

   _____

   _____

3. (a) Why was his mother disappointed? **(Lines 7–13)**
   (b) Why did Max neglect his school work
       (i) in Germany?
       (ii) in Switzerland? **(Lines 13–15)**

   (a) _____

   _____

   (b) (i) _____

   (ii) _____

4. (a) List **three** ways in which Max, Anna and the Zwirn children spent their time. **(Lines 16–17)**
   (b) How did Max and Anna get on with the three Zwirn children? Give details. **(Lines 17–19)**

   (a) _____

   _____

   _____

   (b) _____

   _____

   _____

5. (a) Give **three** details about the new children who arrived on the scene. **(Lines 21–25)**

   (b) Give **two** reasons why the children's game of tag (catch) was more fun than before. **(Lines 28–31)**

(a) _____

_____

_____

(b) _____

_____

Having read the questions, read the whole passage right through at least once. Remember not to worry if you do not understand every word. You will get the gist of the story after a couple of readings and the details will emerge as you work through the questions.

1. This first answer must give *four* details about Anna's last day at school and the information is to be found in the lines 1–4. Start with what you know. You see the familiar words 'Wurst' and 'Brot'. You should have little trouble working out 'sie gingen lachend' and 'machten Pläne für den kommenden Tag'. If you work on the sentences which contain these words, you already have four details without having to understand 'Feier', 'Gesang' or 'Gejodel', all of which could be included. However, even these words should not be impossible to work out. 'Feier'? You may have met 'feiern' (to celebrate) or 'Feiertag' (a public holiday or day of celebration). 'Gesang'? Think of 'singen – sang'. 'Gejodel'? What does it sound like?

    Any *four* of the following would be acceptable answers:
    • A celebration
    • Singing/song
    • Yodelling
    • Each child got a sausage.
    • Each child got a piece of bread.
    • They went (home) laughing (through the village).
    • They made plans for the following day.

2. Here you are asked for *two* things which were different for Max in his school. The source (lines 5–6) is very short. You read that 'Max hatte erst ein paar Tage später frei'. (Max was not free until a few days later./He got his holidays only a few days later.) Here 'erst' means 'not until' or 'only'. His school year did not end with yodelling and sausages, as Anna's did, but rather with reports ('mit Zeugnissen').

Any *two* of the following would be acceptable:
* His holidays started (a few days) later.
* There was no celebration (no yodelling or sausages).
* The pupils got their reports.

3. (a) Why was Max's mother disappointed (lines 7–13)? The previous answer included mention of school reports. You could guess that Max got a bad one. When you examine the text you see the comments 'Strengt sich nicht genug an' and 'Zeigt kein Interesse'. The latter should be very clear to you (shows no interest). The former one means 'does not try hard enough'. You see that his parents were reading his report. There is also a reference to the fact that Max was gifted ('begabt') but did not work ('er arbeitete nur nicht'). Naturally, his mother was disappointed. She had hoped ('hatte gehofft') that he would do better in school in Switzerland than he had done in Germany (lines 11–12).

   In fact, it would probably be easy to answer that Max's mother was disappointed because he got a bad report. However, as you have seen, there is a lot more detail given and you should write as full an answer as you can.

   (b) Why did Max neglect his school work in Germany and in Switzerland (lines 13–15)? These answers are very easy to find. You see 'in Deutschland . . . um Fußball zu spielen' and 'in der Schweiz . . . um zu angeln'.

   Answers:
   (i) to play football
   (ii) to go fishing.

4. (a) Again, this is a straightforward question. You must list *three* ways in which the children spent their time (lines 16–17). You should be able to find the phrases with the three plural verbs '*schwammen* . . . im See', '*spielten* miteinander' and '*gingen* in den Wald'.

   Answers:
   * They swam (in the lake).
   * They played together.
   * They went into the wood/forest.

   (b) You are asked how Max and Anna got on with the three Zwirn children (lines 17–19). The information is contained in two sentences. You see that 'Max verstand sich gut mit Franz' which means that he got on well with him, but the word 'gut' alone should be enough to make the answer obvious. Anna 'hatte Vreneli ganz gern'. (Anna liked Vreneli.) Six-year-old Trudi was not matched with anyone, but 'sie lief immer hinterher' (always ran along behind).

5. (a) *Three* details are needed about the newly arrived children (lines 21–25). You have a wide choice of easy material and should have no difficulty answering.

Any *three* of the following would be acceptable:
- They were a boy and a girl.
- They were German.
- They were about the same age as Max and Anna.
- They were on holidays with their parents.
- They came from Munich.

(b) You are asked for *two* reasons why the game was more fun than before (lines 28–31). The first relevant lines give the information that 'Es hatte früher nie viel Spaß gemacht' (it had never been much fun before) and the reason starts with 'weil' (because). Can you work out 'nur zu viert'? Think of 'vier'. How many children used to play together? Max, Anna, Franz and Vreneli. Poor Trudi did not count 'weil sie nicht schnell genug laufen konnte' (she could not run fast enough). The newly arrived German children were both very fast runners and 'zum ersten Mal war das Spiel wirklich aufregend' (for the first time the game was really exciting).

Your answer could read as follows:
- It was more fun because there were more than four playing.
- The German children ran fast.

 Now test yourself

(Solutions on p. 95)

Answer **in English** the questions which follow the passage.

FREUNDSCHAFT

Alle Mädchen wollen eine beste Freundin. Julia war meine allerbeste Freundin. Wir waren in der gleichen Klasse in der Grundschule, machten unsere Hausaufgaben zusammen, spielten in der Pause zusammen und gingen oft nach der Schule zusammen spazieren. Julia wohnte ganz in der Nähe von mir und manchmal durfte ich bei ihr übernachten. Sie hatte einen älteren Bruder, Gerd. 5
Der erzählte immer lustige Witze und wir haben zusammen viel gelacht.

Wir kamen in die sechste Klasse des Gymnasiums. Julia blieb meine allerbeste Freundin. Eines Tages kam eine neue Schülerin in unsere Klasse. Sie hieß Nadine. Ihre Eltern waren nach Hamburg gezogen, weil ihr Vater eine neue Stelle bekommen hatte. Nadine hatte lange, glatte, blonde Haare und ein 1

---

bildhübsches Gesicht. Sie trug schicke Klamotten. Die Jungen in der Klasse sahen sie bewundernd an und jedes Mädchen wollte ihre Freundin sein.

Nadine saß neben mir im Klassenzimmer und wir wurden langsam gute Freundinnen. Ich war stolz, dass sie mich als Freundin auswählte. Während dieser Zeit wurde Julia ganz ruhig. In der Pause saß sie oft allein auf dem **15** Schulhof und wollte nicht mehr mitspielen. „Lass sie!", sagte einmal Nadine zu mir. „Sie ist so langweilig. Hast du Lust, nach der Schule in die Eisdiele zu gehen?" Meine beste Freundin wollte ich nicht im Stich lassen, aber mit Nadine in die Eisdiele gehen? Das wollte ich sicher! Ich habe ein Schokoladeneis gegessen. Das war auch Julias Lieblingseis. Warum hatte ich sie nicht eingeladen? **20**

Später am Nachmittag ging ich zu ihr nach Hause. Gerd öffnete die Tür. „Hallo, Monika. Lange nicht gesehen", sagte er. „Weißt du, was mit Julia los ist? Sie sitzt nur allein in ihrem Zimmer und weint." Ich schämte mich. Ich wusste, was mit meiner Freundin los war.

Oben in ihrem Zimmer sah ich Julias blasses Gesicht und wusste, dass sie **25** lange geweint hatte. Es fiel mir schwer, ihr ins Gesicht zu gucken, aber Julia fing langsam an zu sprechen. Sie erklärte mir alles. Sie dachte, ich hätte sie nicht mehr gern und das machte sie traurig. „Julia, verzeih mir! Ich war so dumm. Du bist, wie immer, meine allerbeste Freundin", sagte ich. **29**

1. What information is given about the friendship between Julia and the narrator (Monika)? Give **five** details. **(Lines 1–5)**

_____

_____

_____

_____

_____

_____

2. (a) Why did Nadine's family move to Hamburg?   **(Lines 9–10)**
    (b) Describe Nadine's appearance. Give details.   **(Lines 10–11)**
    (a) _____
    (b) _____
         _____

3. (a) Why was the narrator proud?   **(Lines 12–14)**
    (b) How did Julia's behaviour change? Give details.   **(Lines 14–16)**
    (a) _____
         _____
    (b) _____
         _____

4. How did Gerd react when the narrator called? Give details. **(Lines 21–23)**
    _____
    _____

5. (a) Why had Julia been so upset?   **(Line 27–28)**
    (b) Does the story have a happy ending? Explain.   **(Lines 28–29)**
    (a) _____
         _____
    (b) _____
         _____

PAST EXAM QUESTION

(Solutions on p. 98)

Answer **in English** the questions which follow the passage.

Das Gespenst* in der Scheune

Jana und Tim wohnen in der Stadt, in einer Wohnung in einem Hochhaus. In den Ferien fahren sie immer aufs Land und wohnen in einem kleinen Haus in einem Dorf.

Es ist die schönste Zeit im Jahr. Überall sind Berge rund um das Dorf, kleine Berge, auf die man wandern kann. Der Wald und ein See sind auch nicht weit. Im See kann man schwimmen, Boot fahren oder mit einem Schiff einen Ausflug machen. Im Wald sind Hasen und Vögel zu sehen, wenn man leise ist. Man kann auch Himbeeren und Blaubeeren pflücken. Die gibt's dann am Abend zum Abendbrot, wenn alle zusammen nach Hause kommen. Die Eltern haben Zeit. Ein Tag ist so herrlich schön wie der andere.

Aber an manchen Tagen regnet es auch. Dann helfen die Kinder beim Nachbarn, der eine richtige Werkstatt hat, eine Tischlerwerkstatt. Dort bauen sie dann Spielzeuge aus Holz. Oder die Mutter liest ihnen Bücher vor und sie hören gern zu. Oder alle zusammen spielen oder malen etwas. Oder Jana und Tim ziehen Regenjacken an und laufen ins Dorf, wo es andere Kinder gibt.

Am lustigsten ist es bei Ingrid. Sie wohnt in dem kleinen Dorf auf einem Bauernhof. Dort spielen Jana und Tim jedes Jahr in der Scheune. Letzte Woche kam Ingrid und klopfte ganz laut ans Fenster. „Wollt ihr was sehen?" rief sie. „Bei uns in der Scheune ist ein Gespenst* – ganz oben!". Die drei Kinder kletterten die lange Leiter* hinauf. Ingrid legte den Finger auf den Mund: „Pscht! Seid ganz ruhig!" Tim hatte Angst vor dem Gespenst. Die drei starrten ins Dunkel. Da hörten sie etwas. Dann begannen zwei Augen zu glühen: grün und rot, Gespensteraugen. Janas Hals wurde trocken. Tims auch. „Ich will wieder runter", sagte er nervös. Aber aus Angst stieß er an die Leiter. Die Leiter fiel um, und es gab einen lauten Krach. Das Gespenst wurde nervös, es flog über die Köpfe der Kinder. Sie duckten sich und schrien laut: „Hilfe! Hilfe!"

Ingrids Vater hörte die Kinder schreien und lief sofort in die Scheune. Dann sah er es auch: Das Gespenst flatterte jetzt ganz wild umher. Der Vater rief: „Was macht ihr denn da oben? Was ist denn los? Ach, eine Eule ist da! Das arme Tier. Ihr habt es ganz erschreckt!"

* **das Gespenst** = ghost
* **die Leiter** = ladder

1. (a) Where do Jana and Tim live, and (b) where do they spend the holidays?
   (Paragraph 1)

   (a) _____

   _____

   (b) _____

   _____

2. What can one do (a) in the mountains, (b) on the lake and (c) in the forest?
   (Paragraph 2)

   (a) _____

   (b) _____

   _____

   (c) _____

   _____

3. What do Jana and Tim do on rainy days? Give details.   **(Paragraph 3)**

   _____

   _____

   _____

   _____

4. Ingrid came to tell them that there was a ghost in the barn. What did the
   children do in the barn? Give details.   **(Paragraph 4)**

   _____

   _____

   _____

   _____

5. (a) Why did Ingrid's father come into the barn?
   (b) When he saw the owl (the 'ghost'), what did he say to the children?
   (Paragraph 5)

   (a) _____

   (b) _____

Solutions to 'Test Yourself' Questions

A (p. 48)

1. Metzgerei   2. Rolltreppe   3. Einbahnstrasse

B (p. 54)

7	Cruises
3	Hair salon
4	Honey
	Pumpkins
2	Museum open night
1	Candles
6	Television set
	Dressmaker
	Festival
5	Exhibition

C (p. 62)

1. Any visitor to the towns who spends at least one night in Nürnberg or Fürth.
2. Must be under 12 (*end* of twelfth year) and in the company of at least one parent.
3. Any *four* of the following: Visit to all museums (over thirty) in Nürnberg and Fürth; entrance to zoo; entrance to planetarium and other tourist sites; travel on all public transport inside the towns of Nürnberg and Fürth; two postcards and a poster-size photo from the tourist information office, Nürnberg.
4. Any *three* of the following: Many shops in Nürnberg and Fürth; the three tourist information offices; several theatres in both towns; the Paradies Revue Theatre; the IMAX cinema in Nürnberg; guided tours of the towns; trips around the towns.
5. Any *four* of the following: Shopping in the old town; toy museum; zoo; DB (railway) museum; museum for communication.

D (p. 70)

1. (a) Kriegen wir die Arbeiten heute wieder?
2. (c) Schau das im Wörterbuch nach!
3. (d) Morgen fällt die Deutschstunde aus.

E (p. 74)

	Situation	Facilities	Activities	**Two** other details
1	Just outside town	20 single rooms 40 double rooms with shower/ bath	Shopping Bowling	View of castle Good bus con- nection into town Reduction for senior citizens
2	5 minutes' walk from the beach	Rooms with children's beds Large balcony Underground car park Swimming pool	Surfing Swimming Sailing	Child friendly Dog friendly Beautiful view of sea and beach
3	In the middle of the Black Forest	100 beds Room safe Heated swimming pool	Hiking in the forest Excursions in the area Swimming	Quiet area Breakfast buffet on terrace Dog friendly
4	Directly beside the lake	All rooms with bath/shower Sun room Fitness room Parking space	Water sports Cycling	Child friendly Animals not allowed

Note: In the *last* column, any *two* of the details given would be needed.

F (p. 80)
1. Any *four* of the following: Christmas/fir tree; gingerbread; candle light; toys; Christmas carols/songs; presents; love; Christmas is a magical time for children; children look forward to presents at Christmas; they receive presents at Christmas.
2. Any *two* of the following: families are divided; parents are divorced; parents are unemployed; children's wishes remain unfulfilled.
3. (a) Her friends wear fashionable/trendy clothes, they go to concerts, they regularly buy expensive CDs. She has no money for/cannot afford such things.
   (b) Nearly all the pupils in her class have one. If you don't have one, you don't belong to the clique.
4. (a) First he had difficulties in school because he couldn't speak much German. Then his father lost his job and the family is now living on unemployment benefit.
   (b) A portable CD player/a walkman. He would ask the Christchild/baby Jesus.
5. He would like his father to be at home again for Christmas/to be back with his mother and him for Christmas.

G (p. 88)
1. Any *five* of the following: They were best friends; they were in the same primary school class; they did their homework together; played together during the break; often went for a walk together after school; narrator (Monika) sometimes stayed overnight in Julia's house.
2. (a) Her father had got a new job.
   (b) She had long, straight, blond hair and was very pretty/pretty as a picture. She wore trendy/fashionable/chic clothes.
3. (a) Every girl wanted to be Nadine's friend. Nadine had chosen her as a friend./She and Nadine had become friends.
   (b) Julia got rather/very quiet. She often sat alone in the school yard and did not want to play with the others/join in play.
4. He said he had not seen her in a long time. He asked if she knew what was wrong with Julia. He said that Julia was sitting alone in her room, crying.
5. (a) She thought that Monika did not like her any more.
   (b) Yes. Monika asked Julia to forgive her. She said she had been stupid and that Julia was, as always, her very best friend.

Solutions to Past Exam Questions

A (p. 49)

1. Gute Besserung   2. Geschichte   3. Reisebüro

B (p. 56)

2	Wines
6	Riding holidays
5	Health food shop
	Guitar lessons
	Sports gym
1	Children's shoe shop
	Children's party food
7	Second-level school
3	TV magazine
4	Windows and doors

C (p. 64)

1. (a) Any *three* of the following: Discovering the West of Ireland; hiking/hill-walking; cycling; getting to know the country; getting to know the people; environmentally friendly.
   (b) Hear Irish folk/traditional music in friendly pubs.
   (c) In (hospitable) guesthouses/B&Bs.
2. (a) A detached/one-family house in the country.
   (b) Four days and nights a week.
   (c) A car.

D (p. 71)

1. (c) Darf ich das Fenster aufmachen?
2. (b) Schreibt bitte die Hausaufgaben auf!
3. (d) Sei bitte ruhig!

E (p. 75)

	Activity	For whom?	When (day, time)?	Two further details about activity
1	Guided tour of museum	Anyone who would like to know more about fish	Sunday, from 3 p.m.	Offered by Natural History Museum Tour of fish collection Tips and advice from expert
2	Carnival	Children Anyone who enjoys carnival	Sunday, from 11 a.m.	Children can make masks. Children can eat pancakes. There is breakfast for adults. At the checkpoint/ on the Leipziger Straße
3	Dance party	All dance and music fans	Saturday, 8 p.m.– midnight	Entrance costs 5 marks*. World music Money will be sent to a youth project in Rwanda. In the mirrored hall in Karlstraße 7
4	Jazz	Children from age 10	Friday, at 5 p.m.	In the Opera House/on the Behrstraße 55. Entrance is free. Children can play various instruments.

* pre-euro test

Note: In the *last* column, any *two* of the details given would be needed.

F (p. 82)
1. 27 years old; lives near Mainz; is a nurse.
2. Any *four* of the following: Helped build a hospital; helped the doctors; worked in the operating theatre; cooked; handed out food, clothing, toys.
3. (a) 13 weeks.
   (b) Women, small children, old people.
4. Any *five* of the following: Clean water; food; clothing (such as thermal underwear, warm socks, shoes, jackets, pullovers); blankets; nappies; powder; soap.
5. Any *three* of the following: Donate money; work for half a year/6 months at home or abroad; work with the Young Red Cross; work with the Rescue Services; help old or poor people.

G (p. 91)
1. (a) In the town/city, in an apartment block.
   (b) In a small house in a village in the country.
2. (a) Go hiking/walking.
   (b) Swim; go boating; go on an excursion/outing on a ship.
   (c) See hares/rabbits and birds; pick raspberries and blueberries/bilberries.
3. Help the neighbour in his carpentry workshop; make wooden toys; mother reads books to them; play together; paint; put on raincoats; go to the village where there are other children.
4. Climbed up the long ladder. Ingrid put her finger to her mouth/lips and said, 'Ssh . . . Be quiet'. They stared into the dark. Tim said nervously, 'I want to go back down'. Tim knocked against the ladder. They ducked. They shouted 'Help'.
5. (a) He heard the children shout/scream.
   (b) 'What are you doing up there?' 'What's the matter?/ What's wrong?' 'Oh, it's an owl.' 'The poor animal.' 'You frightened it.'

3. WRITTEN EXPRESSION

(80 marks)

This section of the exam may be regarded as the most challenging. It is the only section where you must write in German. Writing is generally the last skill mastered by the language learner. In recognition of this, there are fewer marks awarded in this section. You will find a lot of very useful material in this part of the book to help you gain good marks for your writing.

You have two written tasks on your paper. The longer task is to write a letter in German (minimum 120 words), covering five or six topics. The other task is to write a shorter piece in German in the form of a postcard or a short note.

Vocabulary and suggested sentences for a range of topics are grouped here under the relevant headings. Sample letters, postcards and various types of short notes are included.

Exam Tips

1. Read the questions/guidelines carefully and identify your task. Where a topic is numbered in the letter, make sure to deal with every question or request on that topic. Similarly in the shorter exercise be careful to cover every point.

2. As far as possible try to give equal attention to each topic area. Marks are allotted to each one and if you ignore any topic you will not compensate by writing a full paragraph on another one. An attempt to cover a topic is worthwhile, even if the language you use is poor, as marks are awarded for content as well as for language.

3. Use only words and phrases which you know. For example, if you are asked about hobbies and are not the sporty type, you may still find it useful to say 'Ich bin sehr sportlich. Ich spiele Tennis und Fußball.'

4. If you are asked to write about something specific and you have forgotten the relevant vocabulary, don't panic! Think of a way around the subject. If you have to thank someone for a present and you cannot remember 'das Geschenk', mention the item instead (das Buch, die Schokolade).

5. Keep your writing simple. If you find it difficult to get your message across in one complex sentence, try to break it down into two or three shorter sentences. Instead of 'Ich kann heute Abend nicht ins Kino gehen, weil ich zu viele Hausaufgaben habe,' you could write 'Ich kann heute Abend nicht ins Kino gehen. Ich habe zu viele Hausaufgaben.'

6. In order to maximise your marks you must be as accurate as possible. Be sure to use the correct tenses. Make each verb agree with its subject. Take care with spelling. Remember to start each noun with a capital letter. Pay attention to the rules of word order.

7. Leave some time to look over what you have written. Check grammar and spelling and make sure that you have covered all the necessary points.

KEINE PANIK!

A (Letter)

You already know lots of vocabulary which you could use in the writing section. There is also a wealth of relevant vocabulary under various headings in the Listening Comprehension section of this book. However, you may find it hard to put the words together into good sentences. Here are some helpful ideas.

The first task in this part of your exam is to write a letter in German. This is usually a reply to a German letter which appears on your paper. This may sound difficult, but it is so well structured that it is quite an easy task. First of all you write a suitable greeting and beginning. Then answer the questions asked. A suitable ending will complete the task.

LAYOUT, BEGINNING AND ENDING

It is important to get the layout of a letter right. This is how it should look.

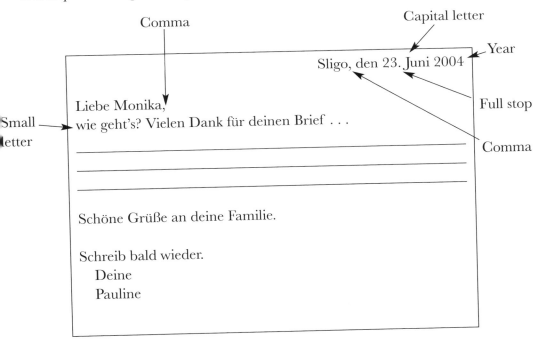

The opening greetings needed are:
- Liebe (feminine)   **Liebe Monika,**
- Lieber (masculine)   **Lieber Stefan,**
- Liebe (plural)   **Liebe Eltern,**

The opening sentence will depend on what is written in the German letter, but could be one of the following:

- **vielen Dank für deinen letzten Brief.** — Thank you very much for your last letter.
- **endlich habe ich Zeit, dir zu schreiben!** — At last I have time to write to you!
- **entschuldige, dass ich nicht früher geschrieben habe.** — Sorry for not writing sooner.
- **es tut mir leid, dass ich erst jetzt schreibe.** — I am sorry that I have not written until now.
- **danke für deinen Brief, den ich heute bekommen habe.** — Thank you for your letter which I received today.
- **ich habe mich über deinen Brief gefreut.** — I was delighted with your letter.
- **wie geht's dir? Hoffentlich gut.** — How are you? Well, I hope.
- **prima, dass du nach Irland kommst.** — It's great that you are coming to Ireland.

Suitable closing sentences include the following:
- **Ich mache jetzt Schluss. Ich muss meine Hausaufgaben machen.** — I'll end now. I have to do my homework.
- **Ich freue mich auf deinen nächsten Brief.** — I am looking forward to your next letter.
- **Ich muss jetzt Schluss machen. Seán ist hier und wir wollen ins Kino.** — I'll have to end now. Seán is here and we are going to the cinema.
- **Ich hoffe, dass ich deine Fragen gut beantwortet habe.** — I hope I have answered your questions well.

- **Schreib bald wieder.** — Write back soon.
- **Lass bald von dir hören.** — Let me hear from you soon.
- **Erzähl mir alles!** — Tell me all.

- **Meine Eltern lassen dich grüßen.** — My parents send their regards.
- **Grüß deine Eltern von mir./Bestell schöne Grüße an deine Eltern.** — Give my regards to your parents.
- **Viele liebe Grüße** — Very best wishes
- **Alles Gute!** — All the best!

- **Bis bald**   Until soon
- **Bis dann**   Until then
- **Tschüss!**   Bye!

Sign off with:
- **Dein** (masculine)
- **Deine** (feminine)

followed by name.

For a *formal letter or note*, use:
- as a greeting:
  Sehr geehrte Damen und Herren,   Dear Sir or Madam,
- formal pronouns:
  Sie, Ihr/Ihre, Ihnen   you, your, to you
- for closing:
  Mit freundlichen Grüßen   Yours sincerely

UNDERSTANDING THE QUESTIONS

The letter on the exam paper includes five or six topics with specific questions. If you answer each question asked, you will find that you have the body of the letter written. You may not recognise what you are being asked in German. Here is a list to remind you of the most frequently used question words.

Wo?	Where?	**Wie viele?**	How many?
Woher?	From where?	**Wie oft?**	How often?
Wohin?	Where to?	**Wie lange?**	How long?
Wann?	When?	**Wer?**	Who?
Was?	What?	**Welcher?** (m.)	Which?/What?
Was für?	What kind of/sort of?	**Welche?** (f.)	
Warum?	Why?	**Welches?** (nt.)	
Wie?	How?	**Welche?** (pl.)	
Wie viel?	How much?		

Examples:

Wie alt bist du?

Ich bin vierzehn Jahre alt.

Wann hast du Geburtstag?

Ich habe am 25. Juli Geburtstag.

Wie siehst du aus?

Ich bin klein. Ich habe lange, schwarze Haare und braune Augen.

Welche Hobbys hast du?

Ich lese gern und ich mag Sport.

Was ist dein Lieblingsfach?

Mein Lieblingsfach ist Deutsch.

Was für Musik hörst du gern?

Ich höre gern Popmusik.

Wo liegt Killarney?

Killarney liegt in Südwestirland.

Sometimes the question does not contain any of these question words. Instead it starts with a verb.

Examples:

Bist du die älteste oder die jüngste in deiner Familie?

Ich bin die älteste in meiner Familie.

Hast du Geschwister?

Ich habe einen Bruder und zwei Schwestern.

Habt ihr ein Haustier?

Wir haben einen Hund.

Gibt es ein Schwimmbad in deiner Stadt?

Ja, es gibt ein neues Schwimmbad in der Stadt.

Kannst du dich beschreiben?

Ich bin klein und habe kurze, lockige Haare.

Sometimes a question is not asked at all. Instead a request is made. Here are some common forms used:

Schreib mir von . . .	Write to me about . . .
Erzähl mir von . . .	Tell me about . . .
Beschreibe . . .	Describe . . .
Schick . . .	Send . . .

Remember that whatever form is used to seek information you should answer as fully as possible.

SAMPLE SENTENCES

The following examples show you how to develop simple answers into more complex ones about basic topics such as yourself, your family, your pets and where you live.

If the letter writer asks you to describe yourself ('Beschreibe dich!'), think of all you can include. As well as the basic physical description (size, hair, eyes) you might say something about your personality, e.g. 'Ich bin freundlich und lustig' (funny); 'Meine Mutter findet mich faul' (lazy). If you want to say that you are an only child ('Ich bin Einzelkind'), you can add a comment or two, e.g. 'Das finde ich gut. Ich bin ein bisschen verwöhnt' (spoiled).

If you are asked about a pet, you already know how to say 'Ich habe einen Hund', but your answer will be much more interesting and will gain you more marks if you add some detail, e.g. 'Er heißt Toby. Er ist klein und schwarz.' (His name is Toby. He is small and black.); 'Ich liebe ihn. Er ist so süß.' (I love him. He is so sweet.); 'Ich gehe oft mit ihm spazieren.' (I often go for a walk with him.)

Here are some extra sentences which you may find useful when writing about *your family*:

Ich habe einen Zwillingsbruder/ eine Zwillingsschwester.	I have a twin brother/sister.
Wir verstehen uns gut.	We get on well.
Wir streiten uns manchmal.	We quarrel sometimes.
Ich komme gut mit meinen Eltern aus.	I get on well with my parents.
Mein Vater ist Geschäftsmann.	My father is a businessman.
Meine Mutter arbeitet in einer Bank.	My mother works in a bank.
Meine Schwester ist verheiratet.	My sister is married.
Sie wohnt nicht mehr bei uns.	She doesn't live with us any more.
Mein Bruder studiert an der Universität in Dublin.	My brother is studying at university in Dublin.

A *description of where you live* could include some of the following sentences:

Ich wohne in einer Großstadt. Sie hat 500 000 Einwohner.	I live in a city. It has 500,000 inhabitants.
Ich wohne in einem Vorort. Hier ist viel los.	I live in a suburb. There is a lot to do/lots happening here.

Wir wohnen in einem Dorf. Es ist schön, aber sehr ruhig.	We live in a village. It is nice but very quiet.
Ich wohne auf dem Land. Meine Eltern mögen es, aber ich finde es langweilig.	I live in the country. My parents like it, but I find it boring.
Hier ist nichts los.	There is nothing to do/nothing happening here.

TOPICS

As stated earlier, the letter requires you to provide information on lots of different subjects. The following examples will help you to approach possible questions and requests with confidence. Remember to check the Listening Comprehension section for any vocabulary you may have forgotten.

House

Kannst du dein Haus beschreiben? Can you describe your house?

Unser Haus ist ganz groß. Es hat zwei Stockwerke.	Our house is quite big. It has two storeys.
Wir haben vier Schlafzimmer, zwei Badezimmer, ein Wohnzimmer, ein Esszimmer und eine Küche.	We have four bedrooms, two bathrooms, a living room, a dining room and a kitchen.

Unsere Oma wohnt bei uns und sie hat ihr eigenes Badezimmer.	Our granny lives with us and she has her own bathroom.
Wir haben auch einen kleinen Garten vor dem Haus.	We also have a small garden in front of the house.
Wir haben eine schöne Aussicht auf die Berge.	We have a beautiful view of the mountains.

Hast du ein eigenes Zimmer? Beschreibe dein Zimmer!	Have you a room of your own? Describe your room.
Zum Glück habe ich ein eigenes Zimmer.	Fortunately, I have a room of my own.
Es ist gemütlich. Die Wände sind weiß angestrichen und der Teppich ist blau.	It is cosy. The walls are painted white and the carpet is blue.
Ich habe einen Kleiderschrank und einen Computer.	I have a wardrobe and a computer.
Ich mache dort meine Hausaufgaben.	I do my homework there.
Leider muss ich mein Zimmer mit meiner kleinen Schwester teilen.	Unfortunately, I have to share my room with my little sister.
Sie ist neun Jahre alt und sie geht mir manchmal auf die Nerven.	She is nine years old and sometimes gets on my nerves.
Der Fußboden ist aus Holz und die Vorhänge sind rosa. Wir haben viele Poster an den Wänden.	The floor is wooden and the curtains are pink. We have lots of posters on the walls.

Wie hilfst du zu Hause?	How do you help at home?
Ich räume mein Zimmer auf.	I tidy my room.
Ich spüle ab. Das finde ich einfach.	I wash up. I find that easy.
Ich bügele. Das ist so langweilig.	I do the ironing. That is so boring.
Ich putze die Fenster. Meine Schwester macht das nie.	I clean the windows. My sister never does that.
Ab und zu koche ich das Abendessen.	Now and then I cook the evening meal.

Sights and Facilities in Your Area

Erzähl mir von deiner Gegend!	Tell me about your area.
Was gibt es in deiner Gegend zu tun?	What is there to do in your area?
Welche Sehenswürdigkeiten gibt es?	What tourist sites are there?

Die Landschaft ist schön/ herrlich.	The countryside is beautiful/ magnificent.
Es gibt einen Wald/Fluss/See.	There is a wood/river/lake.
Man kann angeln/wandern.	One can go fishing/hill-walking.
Das Dorf ist sehr klein. Es gibt nichts für junge Leute.	The village is very small. There is nothing for young people.
Wir fahren am Wochenende oft in die Stadt.	We often go into town at the weekend.

Es gibt ein Schloss/einen Dom.	There is a castle/a cathedral.
Wir haben viele Geschäfte. Man kann gut einkaufen.	We have many shops. It's good for shopping.
Es gibt viele Freizeitmöglichkeiten.	There is a lot to do in your free time.
Wir haben ein neues Hallenbad.	We have a new indoor swimming pool.
Natürlich gibt es auch Kinos und Discos.	Of course, there are also cinemas and discos.

Daily Routine

Beschreibe deinen Alltag!	Describe your daily routine.
Was machst du jeden Tag?	What do you do every day?

Der Wecker klingelt um sieben Uhr.	The alarm clock rings at seven o'clock.
Ich wache um sieben Uhr auf.	I wake up at seven o'clock.
Ich stehe um Viertel nach sieben auf.	I get up at a quarter past seven.
Ich wasche mich./Ich dusche mich.	I wash/have a shower.
Ich ziehe mich an.	I dress myself.
Ich frühstücke gegen acht Uhr.	I have breakfast around eight o'clock.
Dann putze ich mir die Zähne.	Then I clean my teeth.

Ich verlasse das Haus um *halb neun*.	I leave the house at *half past eight*.
Ich fahre mit dem Bus zur Schule.	I go to school on the bus.
Die Fahrt dauert ungefähr zwanzig Minuten.	The journey takes about twenty minutes.
Vor dem Unterricht plaudere ich kurz mit meinen Mitschülern.	Before lessons I chat briefly with my school mates.
Von neun bis vier Uhr bin ich in der Schule.	From nine to four o'clock I am in school.
Ich komme gegen *halb fünf* nach Hause.	I come home around *half past four*.
Ich esse eine Kleinigkeit und mache gleich meine Hausaufgaben.	I have a snack and do my homework straightaway.
Um *halb sieben* gibt es Abendessen bei uns.	We have our evening meal at *half past six*.
Danach sehe ich ein bisschen fern.	After that I watch a little television.
Manchmal gehe ich mit dem Hund spazieren.	Sometimes I go for a walk with the dog.
Gegen zehn Uhr gehe ich ins Bett.	I go to bed around ten o'clock.
Ich lese, bevor ich einschlafe.	I read before I fall asleep.

Hobbies

Was machst du gern in deiner Freizeit?	What do you like to do in your free time?
Erzähl mir von deinen Hobbys!	Tell me about your hobbies.

Ich treibe gern Sport.	I like doing sport.
Am Wochenende spiele ich Fußball.	I play football at the weekend.
Wir trainieren zweimal die Woche beim Sportverein.	We train twice a week at the sports club.
Ich interessiere mich für Musik.	I'm interested in music.
Ich mag Popmusik.	I like pop music.
Ich spiele Klavier.	I play the piano.
Ich bin Mitglied einer Theatergruppe.	I am a member of a theatre/drama group.
Ich lese gern, besonders Romane und Zeitschriften.	I like reading, especially novels and magazines.
Ich sehe nicht besonders gern fern.	I don't particularly like watching television.
Bei schönem Wetter/Wenn das Wetter schön ist, fahre ich gern Rad.	When the weather is fine I like to cycle.

School

Erzähl mir von deiner Schule!	Describe your school.
Wie viele Schüler gehen auf deine Schule?	How many pupils go to your school?
Gibt es Jungen und Mädchen an deiner Schule?	Are there boys and girls at your school?

Unsere Schule ist groß.	Our school is big.
Das Gebäude ist ziemlich modern.	The building is quite modern.
Wir haben viele Klassenzimmer und eine neue Turnhalle.	We have many classrooms and a new gym.
Wir haben 800 Schüler – Jungen und Mädchen.	There are 800 pupils, boys and girls.
Wir haben mehr als 50 Lehrer.	We have over 50 teachers.
Es sind 25 Schüler in meiner Klasse.	There are 25 pupils in my class.

Beschreibe einen typischen Schultag in Irland!	Describe a typical school day in Ireland.
Wann beginnt der Unterricht bei euch?	When do lessons start in your school?
Um wie viel Uhr ist die Schule aus?	What time is school over?
Wie lange dauert eine Unterrichtsstunde?	How long is a lesson?
Wie viele Stunden habt ihr am Tag?	How many classes/lessons have you in the day?
Was machst du während der Mittagspause?	What do you do during the lunch break?

Der Unterricht beginnt um neun Uhr und endet um Viertel vor vier.

Lessons start at 9 o'clock and end at 3.45.

Eine Unterrichtsstunde dauert vierzig Minuten.

One lesson lasts forty minutes.

Wir haben acht Stunden am Tag.	We have eight lessons in the day.
Um elf Uhr haben wir eine kurze Pause und die Mittagspause dauert eine Stunde.	We have a short break at 11 o'clock and the lunch break is one hour long.
Während der Mittagspause esse ich ein Butterbrot und ich trinke Orangensaft.	During the lunch break I eat a sandwich and I drink orange juice.
Ich unterhalte mich mit meinen Freunden.	I chat with my friends.
Manchmal spielen wir Basketball.	Sometimes we play basketball.

Wie viele Fächer hast du?	How many subjects have you?
Was ist dein Lieblingsfach? Warum?	What is your favourite subject? Why?
Welches Fach hast du nicht gern? Warum nicht?	What subject do you not like? Why not?

Ich habe zehn Fächer.	I have ten subjects.
Mein Lieblingsfach ist Mathe.	My favourite subject is maths.
Unsere Lehrerin erklärt alles gut und ich finde es leicht.	Our teacher explains everything well and I find it easy.
Ich habe Erdkunde nicht gern.	I don't like geography.
Man muss so viel lernen und der Lehrer ist sehr streng.	There is so much to learn and the teacher is very strict.

| Wie findest du Deutsch? | How do you find German? |
| Was macht ihr im Deutschunterricht? | What do you do in German class? |

Ich lerne seit drei Jahren Deutsch.	I've been learning German for three years.
Ich mag Deutsch, aber ich finde die Grammatik sehr kompliziert.	I like German but I find the grammar very complicated.
In der Deutschstunde lesen wir Texte und hören deutsche Kassetten.	In German class we read texts and listen to German tapes.
Wir haben dieses Jahr eine deutsche Assistentin.	This year we have a German assistant.

Sie kommt aus Bonn und sie ist sehr freundlich und hilfsbereit.	She comes from Bonn and she is very friendly and helpful.
Natürlich spricht sie viel Deutsch mit uns.	Of course she speaks a lot of German with us.
Ihre Stunden machen uns viel Spaß.	We enjoy her classes a lot.
Wie du siehst, ist mein Deutsch viel besser geworden!	As you see, my German has got a lot better!

Musst du viele Hausaufgaben machen?	Do you have to do a lot of homework?
Wie oft im Jahr bekommt ihr ein Zeugnis?	How often in the year do you get a report?
Was für Noten bekommst du?	What kind of marks do you get?

Ich mache jeden Abend drei Stunden Hausaufgaben.	I do three hours' homework every evening.
Das ist sehr viel. Ich habe dieses Jahr sehr wenig Freizeit.	That's a lot. I have very little free time this year.
Am Wochenende muss ich auch viel lernen.	At the weekend I also have to study a lot.
Nächstes Jahr mache ich das Übergangsjahr. Da gibt's keine große Prüfung.	Next year I am doing Transition Year. There won't be a big exam then.
Wir bekommen dreimal im Jahr ein Zeugnis.	We get a report three times a year.
Ich bekomme immer gute Noten in Mathe, Deutsch und Englisch.	I always get good marks in maths, German and English.
In Erdkunde und Geschichte sind meine Noten immer schlecht.	My marks are always bad in geography and history.
Hoffentlich werde ich im „Junior Cert" nicht durchfallen!	I hope I won't fail my Junior Cert!
In Irisch und Hauswirtschaft bin ich nicht schlecht. Meine Noten sind befriedigend.	I'm not bad at Irish and home economics. My marks are satisfactory.

Wir müssen pünktlich zum Unterricht kommen.	We have to go on time to class.
Wir müssen die Schuluniform tragen.	We have to wear the school uniform.
Wir müssen immer höflich sein.	We must always be polite.
Wir dürfen keinen Schmuck tragen.	We are not allowed to wear jewellery.
Man darf kein Handy im Klassenzimmer benutzen.	We are not allowed to use a mobile phone in the classroom.
Rauchen ist verboten.	Smoking is forbidden.
Kaugummi ist nicht erlaubt.	Chewing gum is not allowed.
Wenn man die Regeln nicht beachtet, muss man zur Schulleiterin gehen.	If you don't observe the rules, you have to go to the principal.
Manchmal muss man nachsitzen.	Sometimes you get detention.

Ist die Schule anders in Irland?   Is school different in Ireland?
Welche Unterschiede gibt es?   What differences are there?
Wie lange sind die Schulferien bei euch?   How long are your school holidays?

Wir müssen hier nicht so früh aufstehen.	We don't have to get up so early here.
Du musst schon um acht Uhr in der Schule sein. Du Arme! (f.)**/ Du Armer!** (m.)	You have to be in school at 8 o'clock. You poor thing!
Wir fangen erst um neun Uhr an.	We don't start until 9 o'clock.
Die Schule ist erst gegen vier Uhr aus.	School is not over until about 4 o'clock.
Aber wir haben samstags keine Schule.	But we don't have school on Saturday.
Du hast es gut! Du hast keinen Nachmittagsunterricht./Du hast den Nachmittag frei.	You're lucky! You have no classes in the afternoon.
In Deutschland habt ihr nur sechs Wochen Sommerferien.	In Germany you only have six weeks' summer holidays.

Wir haben drei Monate im Sommer.	We have three months in summer.
Zu Ostern haben wir meistens zwei Wochen frei.	We usually have two weeks at Easter.
Die Weihnachtsferien dauern zweieinhalb Wochen.	The Christmas holidays are two and a half weeks.
Du hast Glück! Du musst keine Uniform tragen.	You are lucky! You don't have to wear a uniform.
In den meisten irischen Schulen trägt man eine Uniform.	In most Irish schools one wears a uniform.

Beschreibe deine Uniform!	Describe your uniform.
Ich trage einen grünen Rock/ Pullover/Schlips.	I wear a green skirt/jumper/tie.
Ich trage ein weißes Hemd, grüne Strumpfhosen und schwarze Schuhe.	I wear a white shirt, green tights and black shoes.
Ich trage eine graue Hose, einen blauen Pulli, ein graues Hemd, schwarze Socken und schwarze Schuhe.	I wear grey trousers, a blue jumper, a grey shirt, black socks and black shoes.
Ich finde die Uniform hässlich/ altmodisch/praktisch.	I think the uniform is horrible/ old-fashioned/practical.
Ich hasse sie. Sie ist zu warm im Sommer und zu kalt im Winter.	I hate it. It is too warm in summer and too cold in winter.
Ich ziehe mich gleich nach der Schule um.	I change immediately after school.
Ich ziehe eine Jeans und ein T-Shirt an.	I put on jeans and a T-shirt.
Ich trage gern bequeme Klamotten.	I like to wear comfortable clothes.

Erzähl mir von deinem Schulausflug! Wohin seid ihr gefahren? Wie seid ihr gefahren?	Tell me about your school trip. Where did you go? How did you travel?
Am 5. Mai hat unsere Klasse einen Ausflug gemacht.	On 5 May our class went on a trip.
Wir sind mit dem Bus nach Limerick gefahren.	We went by bus to Limerick.
Zuerst sind wir in eine Kunstgalerie gegangen.	First we went to an art gallery.
Das war ein bisschen langweilig.	That was a bit boring.
Danach sind wir einkaufen gegangen.	Afterwards we went shopping.
Ich habe einige Postkarten gekauft.	I bought a few postcards.
Zu Mittag haben wir ein Picknick neben dem Fluss gemacht.	At lunch time we had a picnic beside the river.

Es war richtig schön. Glücklicherweise war das Wetter gut.	It was really nice. Luckily the weather was good.
Später haben wir ein berühmtes Schloss besichtigt.	Later we visited a famous castle.
Das war sehr interessant. Wir sind gegen sechs Uhr nach Hause gekommen.	That was very interesting. We came home around six o'clock.

Student Exchange

Wie ist das Wetter bei euch in Irland?	What is the weather like in Ireland?
Welche Kleider soll ich mitbringen?	What clothes should I bring?
Ich möchte für deine Eltern ein Geschenk kaufen.	I would like to buy a present for your parents.
Kannst du etwas vorschlagen?	Can you suggest something?

Ich freue mich sehr auf deinen Besuch.	I am very much looking forward to your visit.
Du hast nach dem irischen Wetter gefragt.	You asked about the Irish weather.
Das Klima ist mild.	The climate is mild.
Du weißt, dass es hier viel regnet, *nicht nur* im Herbst und im Winter, *sondern auch* im Frühling und im Sommer.	You know that it rains a lot here, *not only* in autumn and in winter *but also* in spring and in summer.
Deshalb nennt man Irland „Die grüne Insel".	That's why Ireland is called 'The Emerald Isle'.
Aber die Sonne scheint auch!	But the sun also shines!
Du sollst Sommerkleidung und Regenkleidung mitbringen.	You should bring summer and rain clothes.
Du willst ein Geschenk für meine Eltern kaufen.	You want to buy a present for my parents.
Das ist sehr nett von dir.	That is very nice of you.
Vielleicht deutsche Kekse oder eine Flasche Wein.	Perhaps some German biscuits or a bottle of wine.

Hoffentlich gefällt dir Irland. I hope you will like Ireland.
Du wirst meine Familie und You will get to know my family and
meine Freunde kennen lernen. friends.
Wir haben einige Ausflüge geplant. We have planned a few trips.
Ich weiß, dass du sportlich bist. I know you're sporty.
Wenn das Wetter schön ist, If the weather is fine we will play
werden wir viel Tennis spielen. a lot of tennis.
Wir werden auch schwimmen gehen. We will also go swimming.

Du hast nach dem irischen Essen You asked about Irish food.
gefragt.
Früher waren Kartoffeln und Potatoes and lamb or bacon and
Lammfleisch oder Speck und cabbage used to be typically Irish.
Kohl typisch irisch.
Heute essen viele Leute gern Today many people like to eat
international, zum Beispiel international food, e.g. Italian or
italienisch oder chinesisch. Chinese.
Mein Lieblingsessen ist Spaghetti My favourite food is spaghetti bolognese.
Bolognese.
Du wolltest wissen, was man in You wanted to know what we
Irland zum Frühstück isst. eat for breakfast in Ireland.
Man isst Spiegelei mit Speck und We eat fried egg with bacon and
Würstchen. sausages.
Das ist typisch irisch, aber wir That is typically Irish but of course
essen das natürlich nicht jeden we don't eat that every day.
Tag.
Das macht dick! That is fattening!
Meistens essen wir nur Cornflakes Usually we eat just cornflakes
oder Toast mit Marmelade. or toast with jam.
Wir trinken Orangensaft, We drink orange juice, tea or coffee.
Tee oder Kaffee.

Freust du dich auf deine Deutschlandreise?	Are you looking forward to your trip to Germany?
Was möchtest du alles machen?	What would you like to do?
Wofür interessierst du dich?	What are you interested in?

Ich freue mich sehr auf meine Deutschlandreise.	I am very much looking forward to my trip to Germany.
Ich war noch nie im Ausland.	I was never abroad before.
Ich möchte mein Deutsch verbessern.	I would like to improve my German.
Ich freue mich darauf, deine Familie kennen zu lernen.	I am looking forward to meeting/ getting to know your family.
Vielleicht könnten wir einen Ausflug in der Gegend machen.	Maybe we could go on a trip in the area.
Gibt es eine Kegelbahn in der Nähe? Oder eine Skateboardanlage?	Is there a bowling alley nearby? Or a skatepark?
Du weißt, wie unternehmungslustig ich bin!	You know how active/adventurous I am!

Hast du deinen Flug gebucht?	Have you booked your flight?
Wann kommst du?	When are you coming?
Um wie viel Uhr kommst du am Flughafen an?	What time are you arriving at the airport?

Ich habe meinen Flug gebucht.	I have booked my flight.
Ich fliege am 3. August nach Wien.	I am flying to Vienna on 3 August.
Ich komme um 14.10 Uhr am Flughafen an.	I am arriving at the airport at 14.10.
Könnt ihr mich abholen oder soll ich mit dem Zug fahren?	Can you collect me or should I take the train?

Bist du gut nach Hause gekommen?	Did you get home safely?
Wie war die Reise?	What was the journey like?
Was hat dir am besten bei uns gefallen?	What did you like best while you were with us?

Ich bin gut nach Hause gekommen.	I got home safely.
Die Reise war sehr angenehm, aber der Flug hatte eine Stunde Verspätung und ich war sehr müde.	The journey was very pleasant but the flight was delayed one hour and I was very tired.
Mein Vater hat mich am Flughafen abgeholt.	My father picked me up at the airport.
Vielen Dank für die schönen Tage bei euch.	Many thanks for the lovely days with you.
Der Besuch hat mir sehr viel Spaß gemacht.	I enjoyed the visit very much.
Ich habe viel Deutsch gelernt.	I learned a lot of German.
Das Essen hat mir sehr gut geschmeckt, besonders der Käsekuchen.	I liked the food a lot, especially the cheesecake.

Am besten hat mir der Ausflug nach Koblenz gefallen.	I liked the trip to Koblenz the best.
Ich lege dir einige Fotos bei.	I'm enclosing some photos.
Ich habe schöne Erinnerungen.	I have lovely memories.

Part-Time Jobs and Money

Hast du einen Nebenjob/Teilzeitjob?	Have you a part-time job?
Was machst du genau?	What do you do exactly?
Wie oft arbeitest du?	How often do you work?
Wie viel Geld verdienst du?	How much money do you earn?
Wie findest du die Arbeit?	How do you find the work?

Ich habe einen Nebenjob.	I have a part-time job.
Ich arbeite jeden Samstag in einem Restaurant.	I work every Saturday in a restaurant.
Ich bediene die Kunden und ich arbeite manchmal in der Küche.	I serve the customers and I sometimes work in the kitchen.
Ich verdiene 8€ die Stunde.	I earn €8 an hour.
Die Arbeit ist ganz interessant, aber manchmal anstrengend.	The work is quite interesting but sometimes demanding.
Ich gehe einmal die Woche bei meinen Nachbarn babysitten.	I babysit once a week for my neighbours.
Sie haben zwei Kinder. Anna ist vier Jahre alt und Daniel ist sieben.	They have two children. Anna is four years old and Daniel is seven.
Die Arbeit ist leicht, weil die Kinder sehr lieb sind.	The work is easy because the children are very sweet.
Ich lese ihnen eine Geschichte vor.	I read them a story.
Wenn sie schlafen, mache ich meine Hausaufgaben.	When they are asleep I do my homework.
Ich verdiene 20€.	I earn €20.
Ich arbeite am Samstag in einem Supermarkt.	I work in a supermarket on Saturday.
Ich fülle die Regale auf.	I stack the shelves.
Ab und zu arbeite ich an der Kasse.	Now and then I work at the checkout.

Ich verdiene 7,50€ pro Stunde.	I earn €7.50 an hour.
Die Arbeit ist nicht schlecht und ich arbeite gern da.	The work is not bad and I like working there.

Wie viel Taschengeld bekommst du?	How much pocket money do you get?
Wofür gibst du dein Geld aus?	What do you spend your money on?
Wofür sparst du?	What are you saving for?

Ich bekomme 15€ die Woche.	I get €15 a week.
Ich bekomme kein Taschengeld.	I don't get any pocket money.
Meine Eltern geben mir Geld, wenn ich es brauche.	My parents give me money whenever I need it.
Ich kaufe CDs und Kredit für mein Handy.	I buy CDs and credit for my mobile phone.
Ich *gebe* mein Geld für Kino und Klamotten *aus*.	I spend my money on the cinema and clothes.
Ich spare für die Ferien/ ein neues Fahrrad.	I am saving for the holidays/a new bicycle.

Holiday Activities

Welche Pläne hast du für die Sommerferien?	What plans have you for the summer holidays?
Fährst du in Urlaub? Ins Ausland?	Are you going on holiday? Abroad?
Bleibst du in Irland?	Are you staying in Ireland?

Nach der Prüfung werde ich mich ausruhen.	I am going to relax after the exam.
Wir machen im Juli einen Familienurlaub.	We are going on a family holiday in July.
Wir fahren nach Frankreich.	We are going to France.
Wir machen einen Campingurlaub in der Nähe von Carnac.	We are going on a camping holiday near Carnac.
Wir fahren dieses Jahr nicht ins Ausland.	We are not going abroad this year.
Wir haben ein Ferienhaus in Donegal.	We have a holiday home in Donegal.

Wir werden dort einen Monat verbringen.	We are going to spend a month there.
Ich freue mich darauf.	I am looking forward to it.
Ich fahre im August in die „Gaeltacht" in Galway.	In August I am going to the 'Gaeltacht' in Galway.
Das ist eine Gegend, wo man nur Irisch spricht.	That is an area where only Irish is spoken.
Ich will meine Irischkenntnisse verbessern.	I want to improve my Irish.
Wie du weißt, ist Irisch bei uns Pflichtfach.	As you know Irish is a compulsory subject for us.
Im Juli mache ich einen Deutschkurs.	I am doing a German course in July.
Ich hoffe, mein Deutsch zu verbessern.	I hope to improve my German.
Ich werde in einem Internat wohnen.	I will stay in a boarding school.

Was hast du letzten Sommer gemacht?	**What did you do last summer?**
Letzten Sommer bin ich in Irland geblieben.	Last summer I stayed in Ireland.
Das Wetter war herrlich.	The weather was wonderful.
Ich habe einen Sportkurs gemacht.	I did a sports course.
Wir sind nach Portugal geflogen.	We flew to Portugal.
Wir haben ein Auto gemietet.	We hired a car.
Wir sind zwei Wochen in einem Hotel geblieben.	We stayed in a hotel for two weeks.
Die Sonne hat jeden Tag geschienen.	The sun shone every day.

Was hast du für die Weihnachtsferien vor?	What have you planned for the Christmas holidays?
Wie feiert man Weihnachten in Irland?	How do you celebrate Christmas in Ireland?

Wir bekommen zweieinhalb Wochen Ferien.	We get two and a half weeks' holidays.
Unser Opa kommt zu Besuch und bleibt eine Woche bei uns.	Our grandfather is coming to visit and is staying a week with us.
Ich werde für meine Familie und meine Freunde viele Geschenke kaufen.	I will buy lots of presents for my family and my friends.
Meine Freunde und ich gehen Schlittschuh laufen.	My friends and I are going ice-skating.
In Irland feiert man Weihnachten mit der Familie.	In Ireland we celebrate Christmas with the family.
Wir haben einen Weihnachtsbaum und viel Weihnachtsschmuck im Haus.	We have a Christmas tree and a lot of Christmas decorations in the house.
Am Heiligabend gehen wir in die Kirche und singen Weihnachtslieder.	On Christmas Eve we go to church and sing Christmas carols.

Am 25. Dezember gibt es ein großes Mittagessen mit Truthahn, Schinken, Rosenkohl, Kartoffeln und Möhren.	On 25 December there is a big dinner with turkey, ham, Brussels sprouts, potatoes and carrots.
Jedes Jahr backt meine Mutter einen großen Kuchen.	Every year my mother bakes a big cake.
Der schmeckt immer lecker.	It always tastes delicious.
Es ist sehr gemütlich.	It is very cosy.

Was hast du während der Osterferien gemacht?	What did you do during the Easter holidays?
Erzähl mir von deinen Osterferien!	Tell me about your Easter holidays.

Wir hatten zwei Wochen Ferien.	We had two weeks' holidays.
Ich bin zu Hause geblieben.	I stayed at home.
Ich habe ferngesehen und am Computer gespielt.	I watched television and played on the computer.
Natürlich habe ich viele Ostereier gegessen.	Of course I ate a lot of Easter eggs.
Ich bin mit meinen Freunden in die Stadt gegangen.	I went into town with my friends.
Wir haben einen Stadtbummel gemacht.	We went for a stroll around the town.

Birthdays

Wie hast du deinen Geburtstag gefeiert?	How did you celebrate your birthday?
Hast du eine Party gehabt?	Did you have a party?
Welche Geschenke hast du bekommen?	What presents did you get?

Du wolltest wissen, wie ich meinen Geburtstag gefeiert habe.	You wanted to know how I celebrated my birthday.
Es gab eine tolle Party bei mir.	There was a great party at my house.
Meine Mutter hat einen Geburtstagskuchen gebacken.	My mother baked a birthday cake.
Ich hatte vierzehn Kerzen darauf.	I had fourteen candles on it.
Ich habe zwölf Freunde eingeladen.	I invited twelve friends.
Wir haben viel gegessen und getrunken.	We ate and drank a lot.
Ich habe viele schöne Geschenke bekommen.	I got a lot of lovely presents.
Meine Eltern haben mir ein Handy geschenkt.	My parents gave me a mobile phone as a present.
Ich habe viele Computerspiele geschenkt bekommen.	I got a lot of computer games as presents.
Später haben wir Musik gehört und viel getanzt.	Later we listened to music and danced a lot.
Vielen Dank für das Geschenk.	Thank you for the present.
Die CD ist eine tolle Überraschung.	The CD is a wonderful surprise.
Ich habe mich darüber gefreut.	I was thrilled with it.
Er/Sie ist mein/e Lieblingssänger/in.	He/She is my favourite singer.
Ich mag das T-Shirt. Es passt mir sehr gut.	I like the T-shirt. It fits me very well.
Die Farbe steht mir gut.	The colour suits me.
Blau ist meine Lieblingsfarbe.	Blue is my favourite colour.

Concert

Du hast geschrieben, dass du in ein Konzert gegangen bist.	You wrote that you went to a concert.
Was für ein Konzert war das?	What kind of concert was it?
Schreib mir davon!	Write to me about it.

Ich war am 17. Mai mit drei Freunden bei einem Rockkonzert.

I was at a rock concert with three friends on 17 May.

Die Kool Kats waren prima.

The Kool Kats were brilliant.

Sie haben alle ihre Hits gesungen. They sang all their hits.

Die Stimmung war wirklich toll. The atmosphere was really great.

Ich bin mit meinen Eltern in ein klassisches Konzert in der Konzerthalle gegangen.

I went to a classical concert in the concert hall with my parents.

Es hat vor vier Wochen stattgefunden.

It took place four weeks ago.

Ein Jugendorchester aus der Gegend hat gespielt.

A youth orchestra from the area played.

Es war wunderbar.

It was wonderful.

Football Match

Du hast mir kurz gesagt, dass du zu einem Fußballspiel gegangen bist.	You mentioned briefly that you went to a football match.
Erzähl mir davon!	Tell me about it.
Wo war das?	Where was it?
Wie war das?	How was it?

Ich bin mit meinem Bruder Paul zu einem Fußballspiel in Croke Park gegangen.

I went to a football match in Croke Park with my brother Paul.

Das ist ein großes Stadion in Dublin.

That is a big stadium in Dublin.

Unsere Mannschaft hat gegen eine andere Grafschaft gespielt.

Our team played against another county.

Es waren über 40 000 Zuschauer dort und die Atmosphäre war fantastisch.

There were over 40,000 spectators and the atmosphere was fantastic.

Das Spiel war spannend und wir haben gewonnen.

The match was exciting and we won.

Illness and Accidents

Du hast geschrieben, dass du krank warst.	You wrote that you were ill.
Was hattest du?	What was wrong with you?
Wie geht's dir jetzt?	How are you now?

Du wolltest wissen, was mit mir los war.

You wanted to know what was wrong with me.

Ich fühlte mich nicht wohl.

I didn't feel well.

Ich konnte nichts essen und ich war sehr schwach.

I couldn't eat anything and I was very weak.

Ich hatte auch hohes Fieber.

I also had a high temperature.

Meine Mutter war besorgt und sie hat den Arzt angerufen.

My mother was worried and she rang the doctor.

Ich hatte nämlich die Grippe und ich musste vier Tage im Bett bleiben.

I actually had the flu and had to stay in bed for four days.

Es geht mir jetzt viel besser, danke, und ich gehe wieder zur Schule.

I'm much better now, thank you, and I'm back at school.

Du hast mir kurz gesagt, dass deine Oma im Krankenhaus war. Wie lange war sie dort? Wie geht's ihr jetzt?	You mentioned that your granny was in hospital. How long was she there? How is she now?

Meine Oma war krank. Sie war zwei Wochen im Krankenhaus, aber sie ist jetzt wieder zu Hause.
Es geht ihr viel besser./Sie ist wieder gesund.
Ich habe sie am Wochenende besucht.

My granny was ill. She was in hospital for two weeks but she is back home again.
She is much better./She is well again.

I visited her at the weekend.

Du hast mir geschrieben, dass dein Bruder einen Unfall hatte. Was ist passiert? Musste er ins Krankenhaus? Wie geht's ihm jetzt?	You wrote that your brother had an accident. What happened? Did he have to go to hospital? How is he now?

Mein Bruder Conor ist im März vom Fahrrad gefallen.
Er hat sich das Bein gebrochen und musste mit dem Krankenwagen ins Krankenhaus.
Er muss einen Gips tragen und geht noch auf Krücken.
Er langweilt sich im Haus und ist oft schlecht gelaunt, weil er nicht Fußball spielen kann.

My brother Conor fell off his bicycle in March.
He broke his leg and had to go to hospital by ambulance.

He has to wear a plaster cast and is still on crutches.
He is bored in the house and is often in a bad mood because he can't play football.

You have received a letter from your Swiss exchange partner. Write a letter in reply, answering all the questions (which have been numbered for you) in some detail. **(120 words minimum)**

Luzern, den 7. Juni 2003

Liebe/r .... ,

ich habe lange nichts mehr von dir gehört und habe mir gedacht, ich schreibe dir doch mal wieder. Ich hätte dir am liebsten eine E-Mail geschickt, weiß aber deine E-Mail Adresse nicht. Ich verbringe im Moment viel Zeit an meinem Computer – mindestens 2 Stunden am Tag. Das ist mein Hobby. **(1)** Was machst du denn gerne in deiner Freizeit? Wie oft und wo machst du das?

Du hast mir geschrieben, dass du in einem Haus wohnst. **(2)** Kannst du dein Haus beschreiben? Wie viele Zimmer habt ihr? Habt ihr einen Garten? Wir wohnen in einem Wohnblock in der Stadtmitte von Luzern. Die Wohnung ist recht klein, aber ich habe mein eigenes Zimmer. Ich lege dir ein paar Fotos bei. Leider sind Haustiere nicht erlaubt. Du hast neulich geschrieben, ihr wolltet ein Haustier kaufen. **(3)** Was für ein Tier ist das? Kannst du es mir beschreiben? Wie teuer war es?

Schreib mir von dem Sprachkurs, den du gemacht hast. **(4)** Wann und wo war das genau? Was habt ihr alles im Kurs gemacht?

Ich möchte deiner Familie dieses Jahr etwas zu Weihnachten aus der Schweiz schicken. Ich weiß aber nicht, was. **(5)** Was denkst du? Kannst du mir ein paar Tipps geben? Bitte schreib diesmal schneller zurück!

Tschüss,

dein(e)
Kai

P.S. Meine E-Mail Adresse ist: k.beil@freenet.ch

As you see, the topics are numbered and you are required to answer them 'in some detail'. Let's look closely at the five topics.

1. The topic is free time and there are actually *three* questions to be answered:
   - **Was** machst du gerne in deiner Freizeit?
   - **Wie oft** und **wo** machst du das?

Notice you are not simply required to say *what* your hobbies are but also *how often* and *where* you practise them.

Was machst du gerne in deiner Freizeit? You have lots of possibilities: 'Ich treibe gern Sport./Ich bin sehr sportlich./Ich spiele gern Tennis, Fußball, Basketball./Ich lese gern./Ich verbringe auch viel Zeit am Computer./Ich höre gern Musik./Ich spiele Klavier.'

Elaborate a little on one or two hobbies. If you like reading, say what kind of books/magazines you like: 'Ich lese besonders gern Romane/Krimis/Modezeitschriften.' For television you could say: 'Ich sehe gern fern, besonders Serien./Meine Lieblingssendung ist „The Simpsons".' To say more about music you could say: 'Meine Lieblingsgruppe sind The Corrs.'

Remember you still have two more questions to answer on this topic.

Wie oft machst du das? Short simple answers are sufficient here. Think logically and remember the vocabulary you have that can be used appropriately. In the case of sport, you might play once or twice a week ('einmal/zweimal die Woche') or at the weekend ('am Wochenende') or during the holidays ('in den Ferien'). Some might be daily or almost daily activities, e.g. 'jeden Tag', 'jeden Abend', 'fast jeden Abend': 'Ich höre jeden Abend Musik./Fast jeden Tag spiele ich am Computer.'

Wo machst du das? 'Zu Hause/in meinem Zimmer/in der Schule/in einem Sportverein (sports club)/in der Stadt.'

2. In the second topic area, your house, there are *three* questions:
   - Kannst du dein Haus **beschreiben**?
   - **Wie viele** Zimmer habt ihr?
   - Habt ihr einen **Garten**?

Describing your house should not be a difficult task. Is it a bungalow, a detached house, a semi-detached house, a terraced house? 'Es ist ein Bungalow/ein Einfamilienhaus/ein Doppelhaus/ein Reihenhaus.' 'Ich wohne in einem Bungalow/in einem Einfamilienhaus/in einem Doppelhaus/in einem Reihenhaus.' 'Es ist groß/klein/modern.'

Say where it is: 'auf dem Land/in der Stadt/in der Nähe von . . .'.

Wie viele Zimmer habt ihr? While the letter is written to you and uses 'du', 'dir', 'dein', it includes questions like this one which is addressed to you and your family: Habt *ihr*? (*you:* plural informal). It is best to answer with 'wir' (we): 'Wir haben drei/vier Schlafzimmer, ein Wohnzimmer, ein Badezimmer, ein Esszimmer', etc.

Use some adjectives: 'ein kleines Zimmer', 'eine große Küche'. If you find adjective endings difficult, you can sometimes avoid them, e.g. 'Das Esszimmer ist klein./Die Küche ist groß.'

React to the photos sent: 'Danke für die Fotos. Sie sind schön.' Say if you have your own room as Kai has: 'Ich habe auch ein eigenes Zimmer./Ich teile mein Zimmer mit meiner Schwester/meinem Bruder.' Include a few words about it: 'schön', 'gemütlich'.

Habt ihr einen **Garten**? 'Ja, wir haben einen Garten. Er ist vor/hinter dem Haus und ist ziemlich groß/klein/schön.' Think of the vocabulary you have which could be used to develop this answer. Flowers, trees, vegetables ('Blumen, Bäume, Gemüse')? Perhaps you could say who likes to work there: 'Mein Vater arbeitet gern dort.'

3. The next topic is your pet. Once again, there are *three* specific questions:
   • **Was für** ein Tier ist das?
   • Kannst du es mir **beschreiben**?
   • **Wie teuer** war es?

The first question, **Was für** ein Tier? (What kind of animal?), is straightforward but before you choose a pet be careful that you have the vocabulary to answer the second question where you are required to describe it. A dog, for example, might give you more scope for vocabulary than a goldfish: 'Wir haben einen Hund bekommen.'

Kannst du es mir **beschreiben**? 'Er ist ein Labrador/ein Terrier/ein Mischling (mongrel) und heißt . . . Er ist sehr freundlich/süß/ist . . . Jahre alt/hat lange Ohren.' Perhaps you like to take him for a walk: 'Ich gehe gern mit ihm spazieren.'

'**Wie teuer** war es?' might be difficult if you are not familiar with the cost of pets. If you know or can make a logical guess, use: 'Er/Sie/Es hat . . . Euro gekostet' or 'Er/Sie/Es war nicht teuer – nur . . . Euro'. To avoid giving a specific price but to make sure you answer the question, you could say: 'Der Hund war ein Geschenk von meinem Onkel/einem Freund/einer Freundin./Unser Nachbar (neighbour) hat uns den Hund geschenkt/ gegeben./Wir haben einen Hund von Opa geschenkt bekommen.'

4. The fourth topic is your language course and here again there are *three* pieces of information required:

- **Wann** und **wo** war das genau?
- **Was** habt ihr alles im Kurs gemacht?

Remember Kai's letter was written in June (see date on letter above). The questions asked refer to the past. The course might have been at Easter, but was more likely during the summer. Therefore, you should write about a course you did 'zu Ostern' or 'letzten Sommer', for example: 'Ich habe letzten Sommer einen Irisch-/Deutschkurs gemacht./Ich habe zu Ostern an einem Französischkurs teilgenommen.'

Wann und wo war das **genau**? You are asked to be exact. **Wann**? 'Das war Anfang Juli und hat drei Wochen gedauert./Der Kurs hat vom 10. bis zum 15. April gedauert.'

Wo? 'Ich bin nach Donegal gefahren. Das liegt in Nordwestirland./Ich bin in die „Gaeltacht" gefahren.' You would need to explain to your Swiss exchange partner what that is! 'Das ist eine Gegend, wo man Irisch spricht.'

Or you could say 'Ich bin in eine Sprachschule in Dublin gegangen, um mein Deutsch zu verbessern.'

Was habt ihr . . . gemacht? 'Wir sind in den Deutsch-/Irischunterricht gegangen./Wir hatten jeden Tag drei Stunden Deutsch/Irisch./Wir durften nur Deutsch/Irisch sprechen./Wir haben nur . . . gesprochen./ Wir haben deutsche/ irische Lieder gelernt/gesungen./Wir haben Tennis gespielt und einige Ausflüge gemacht.'

Add a comment: 'Es hat mir viel Spaß gemacht./Ich habe viel Deutsch/Irisch gelernt.'

5. Here you are asked to suggest a suitable Christmas present for your family that your exchange partner would like to send from Switzerland:

- Was **denkst** du?
- Kannst du mir ein paar **Tipps** geben?

First, show your appreciation: 'Du willst uns etwas zu Weihnachten schicken. Das ist sehr nett von dir.'

Tipps? You may have ideas on what you would like to receive from Switzerland, but again, keep within the range of your vocabulary. Perhaps you could use 'Schweizer Schokolade' (Swiss chocolate), 'ein Buch über die Schweiz' (a book about Switzerland), 'ein Bild' (a picture), or 'Weihnachtsschmuck aus der Schweiz' (Swiss Christmas decoration).

Here are two sample answers.

Tara, den 14. Juni 2003

Liebe Kai,

diesmal schreibe ich schneller zurück! Ich beantworte gerne deine Fragen. Ich habe auch einen Computer zu Hause. Aber das ist nicht mein Lieblingshobby. Ich interessiere mich mehr für Sport. Ich spiele zweimal die Woche in einem Tennisverein. Basketball finde ich auch gut, aber das spiele ich nur in der Schule, in der Sportstunde. Ich höre auch gern Musik. Ich mag Westlife. Sind sie in der Schweiz bekannt?

Ich wohne in einem Einfamilienhaus auf dem Land. Es ist ziemlich groß. Wir haben vier Schlafzimmer, ein Wohnzimmer, eine große Küche und ein Badezimmer. Wir haben auch einen Garten, wo mein Vater gern am Wochenende arbeitet.

Danke für die Fotos. Du hast ein schönes Zimmer. Ich habe auch mein eigenes Zimmer. Es ist schön und gemütlich. Ich mache dort meine Hausaufgaben. Unser Haustier hat nichts gekostet. Wir haben von unserem Onkel einen Hund geschenkt bekommen. Er ist ein kleiner Mischling und heißt Bruno. Er ist braun und weiß. Wir finden ihn so lieb und mein Bruder Kenneth geht fast jeden Tag mit ihm spazieren.

Du hast nach meinem Sprachkurs gefragt. Ich habe letzten Sommer einen Irischkurs gemacht. Du weißt, Irisch ist bei uns Pflichtfach in der Schule. Ich bin für drei Wochen in die „Gaeltacht" in Donegal in Nordwestirland gefahren. Die „Gaeltacht" ist eine Gegend, wo man nur Irisch spricht. Wir hatten jeden Tag Irischunterricht und wir mussten die ganze Zeit Irisch sprechen. Es hat Spaß gemacht. Wir haben irische Lieder gelernt. Ich habe nette Leute kennen gelernt.

Du denkst schon an Weihnachten! Ich finde es sehr nett, dass du uns etwas schicken willst. Vielen Dank! Vielleicht könntest du uns einen Kalender mit Bildern aus der Schweiz schicken. Ich möchte ein Poster aus der Schweiz für mein Zimmer. Oder Schokolade vielleicht? Meine ganze Familie mag Schokolade.

Also Kai, ich mache jetzt Schluss und freue mich auf deinen nächsten Brief. Bitte grüß deine Eltern von mir.

Schreib bald wieder!
Deine
Susan

Galway, den 27. Juni 2003

Lieber Kai,
danke für deinen netten Brief. Endlich habe ich Zeit, dir zu schreiben. Ich musste für meine Prüfungen sehr viel lernen.

Du hast viele Fragen. Zuerst schreibe ich über meine Hobbys. Ich verbringe auch viel Zeit am Computer in meinem Zimmer und habe viele Computerspiele. Abends lese ich auch sehr gern, besonders Krimis. Ich schwimme fast jeden Tag im Sommer. Wenn das Wetter schön ist, schwimme ich in der See und wenn es schlecht ist, gehe ich ins Hallenbad.

Ich wohne in einem Doppelhaus am Stadtrand. Wir haben oben drei Schlafzimmer und ein Badezimmer. Unten gibt es ein Wohnzimmer, eine Küche und ein kleines Esszimmer. Danke für die Fotos. Dein Zimmer ist sehr schön. Du hast Glück! Ich muss mein Zimmer mit meinem Bruder teilen.

Wir haben einen kleinen Garten mit Blumen. Leider haben wir nicht genug Platz für einen Hund. Deshalb haben wir ein Kaninchen gekauft. Es hat 20€ gekostet. Es ist klein, schwarz und sehr süß. Es heißt Trixi.

Ich erzähle dir jetzt von meinem Sprachkurs. In den Osterferien habe ich einen Französischkurs in einer Internatschule gemacht. Die Schule liegt ganz in der Nähe. Wir hatten jeden Tag vier Stunden Französisch und wir mussten Französisch sprechen. Wir haben viele Vokabeln gelernt und einen guten Film gesehen.

Du willst meiner Familie etwas zu Weihnachten schicken. Danke schön! Das finde ich sehr nett, aber auch lustig. Ich kaufe meine Geschenke erst im Dezember! Vielleicht kannst du uns ein Buch mit Fotos von der Schweiz schicken. Die Landschaft ist so schön. Natürlich essen wir alle gern Bonbons und Schokolade.

Schöne Grüße an deine Familie.

Bis bald!
    Dein
    Peter

You have recently received a letter from your German exchange partner. Write a letter in reply, answering all the questions (which have been numbered for you) in some detail. **(120 words minimum)**

Cuxhaven, den 26. Mai 2004

Liebe/r ....,

ich finde es klasse, dass du mit deinen Eltern im Sommer nach Deutschland kommst. Ich freue mich schon total darauf, dich zu sehen. **(1)** Wann kommt ihr denn genau? Kommt ihr mit der Fähre oder dem Flugzeug? Wie lange dauert die Reise eigentlich?

Du weißt sicher schon, wo ihr übernachtet. **(2)** Habt ihr schon ein Hotel oder eine andere Unterkunft gebucht? Bei uns ist auch Platz zum Übernachten, wenn ihr wollt. Was meinst du? **(3)** Wollt ihr ein Auto mieten oder bringt ihr das eigene Auto?

Wenn meine Eltern und ich Urlaub machen, machen wir immer Aktivurlaub. **(4)** Wie ist es denn in deiner Familie? Was wollt ihr hier in Deutschland alles machen?

Ich habe letzte Woche mein Zeugnis bekommen. Die Noten waren nicht besonders gut und meine Eltern waren richtig sauer! **(5)** Was für Noten bekommst du normalerweise in der Schule? Was ist dein Lieblingsfach, und warum? Welches Fach machst du nicht so gern? Warum nicht?

Du warst doch letzte Woche beim Robbie Williams Konzert, oder? **(6)** Wo war das nochmal? Wie bist du dort hingekommmen? Wie hast du das Konzert gefunden? Ich finde die Musik von Robbie super!

Das wär's für heute.
Viel Spaß beim Urlaub planen!

    Dein(e)
    Michi

Here are two sample answers.

Drogheda, den 12. Juni 2004

Lieber Michi,

danke für deinen Brief. Wie geht's? Mir geht's gut. Ich freue mich auf unsere Reise nach Deutschland. Nur noch fünf Wochen! Wir fahren am 18. Juli mit der Fähre nach Cherbourg. Die Reise dauert sehr lange, mehr als zwanzig Stunden. Hoffentlich werde ich nicht seekrank! Dann fahren wir weiter nach Deutschland.

Wir hoffen, am 20. Juli in Deutschland anzukommen. Vielen Dank für die Einladung, bei euch zu übernachten, aber wir haben schon ein Hotel in Cuxhaven gebucht. Wir bringen unser eigenes Auto mit. Meine Eltern finden das sehr praktisch. Vielleicht können wir uns am 21. Juli treffen. Ich rufe dich an. Ich freue mich sehr darauf.

Wir möchten am 23. Juli nach Berlin fahren und wir werden dort eine Woche verbringen. Da gibt es etwas für die ganze Familie. Meine Eltern interessieren sich für Kunst und sie wollen Kunstgalerien besuchen. Meine Schwester möchte einkaufen gehen. Es gibt tolle Geschäfte in Berlin. Ich möchte die historischen Gebäude besichtigen.

Mein Lieblingsfach in der Schule ist Geschichte. Ich finde das Fach sehr interessant und ganz einfach. Schade, dass dein Zeugnis nicht so gut war. Ich bekomme normalerweise gute Noten in Geschichte, Deutsch und Irisch, aber in Mathe bekomme ich immer schlechte Noten. Ich finde Mathe sehr schwierig und ich kann den Lehrer nicht verstehen.

Du hast nach dem Konzert gefragt. Es hat in einer großen Konzerthalle in Dublin stattgefunden. Ich bin mit dem Zug nach Dublin gefahren. Es war einfach klasse! Robbie hat alle seine Hits gesungen. Wenn er in Deutschland ein Konzert gibt, musst du dort hingehen.

Ich mache jetzt Schluss. Meine Eltern lassen dich grüßen.

Tschüss!
    Dein
    David

Kilkenny, den 6. Juni 2004

Liebe Michi,

schönen Dank für deinen Brief, den ich letzte Woche bekommen habe. Ich finde es sehr schön, dass wir uns endlich treffen werden.

Meine Mutter hat den Flug gebucht. Wir fliegen am 26. Juni nach Frankfurt. Der Flug dauert zweieinhalb Stunden. Meine Mutter hat eine Freundin in der Nähe von Frankfurt und wir werden ein paar Tage bei ihr verbringen. Nachher wollen wir ein Auto mieten und einige Städte am Rhein besichtigen. Meine Eltern haben Hotels gebucht. Ich weiß nicht genau, wo. Es ist sehr nett von dir, uns einzuladen, aber sie haben schon ein Hotel in Cuxhaven gebucht.

Meine Familie ist auch ganz aktiv. Alle treiben gern Wassersport. Wir segeln sehr gern. Wenn das Wetter gut ist, werde ich sicher schwimmen. Wir haben auch vor, eine Schifffahrt auf dem Rhein zu machen. Ich weiß, dass die Landschaft dort sehr schön ist.

Du hast von deinem Zeugnis geschrieben. Ich bekomme diesen Sommer kein Zeugnis, weil ich mein „Junior Cert" mache. Normalerweise bekomme ich gute Noten in Kunst. Das ist mein Lieblingsfach. Ich zeichne und male sehr gern. Ich kann Irisch nicht leiden. Ich finde die Grammatik zu kompliziert und meine Noten in Irisch sind immer schlecht. In den anderen Fächern sind meine Noten meistens befriedigend.

Das Robbie Williams Konzert war prima! Es war in einer Konzerthalle in Belfast. Ich war mit zwei Freundinnen da. Wir sind mit dem Bus hingefahren. Wir waren ganz vorne in der Halle und konnten Robbie sehr gut sehen. Er war wirklich toll. Ich erzähle dir alles, wenn wir uns in Cuxhaven treffen. Ich freue mich sehr auf meinen Besuch.

Viele liebe Grüße

    Deine
    Aoife

B (Shorter Exercise)

The other task in this section of your exam is to write a short note or a postcard. The instructions and the guidelines are given in English. Examples of what you may be asked to write here include:

- A holiday postcard
- A phone message
- A notice for a notice board
- A greeting card for a special occasion
- A get-well-soon wish
- A note about travel arrangements
- An invitation
- A thank-you note
- A regret/apology/cancellation
- A note to explain absence
- A request to a penpal
- A formal request for information
- A formal booking.

TOPICS

Holidays

Grüße aus . . .!	Greetings from . . .!
Ich bin hier in Italien/Wien/ Südfrankreich/im Schwarzwald.	I am here in Italy/Vienna/the south of France/the Black Forest.
Ich verbringe zwei Wochen mit meiner Familie in Spanien.	I am spending two weeks in Spain with my family.
Es macht mir viel Spaß.	I'm having great fun.
Es gibt viel zu tun.	There is a lot to do.
Die Leute sind freundlich.	The people are friendly.
Ich vermisse dich./Du fehlst mir.	I miss you.
Ich finde den Ort sehr langweilig.	I find the place very boring.
Ich langweile mich.	I am bored.
Es gibt nichts zu tun.	There is nothing to do.

Das Wetter ist	**prima.**	great
	furchtbar	terrible
	sonnig	sunny
	regnerisch	rainy

Es ist sehr	**warm.**	warm
	kalt	cold
	heiß	hot
	bewölkt	overcast

Wir haben Glück mit dem Wetter.	We are lucky with the weather.
Die Sonne scheint jeden Tag.	The sun shines every day.
Wir haben Pech mit dem Wetter.	We are unlucky with the weather.
Es ist kalt und windig.	It is cold and windy.
Es gibt Gewitter.	There are thunderstorms.

Wir machen einen Skiurlaub.	We are on a skiing holiday.
Der Schnee ist herrlich.	The snow is wonderful.
Ich lerne viel Französisch/ Deutsch/Italienisch.	I'm learning a lot of French/German/ Italian.
Ich schwimme fast jeden Tag.	I swim nearly every day. The sea is
Die See ist schön warm.	nice and warm.
Mein Vater läuft Wasserski.	My father goes water-skiing.

Gestern haben wir ein Boot gemietet.	Yesterday we hired a boat.
Wir sind zu einer kleinen Insel gefahren.	We went out to a small island.
Am Montag haben wir einen Ausflug nach Rom/Freiburg/ Rennes gemacht.	On Monday we went on a trip to Rome/Freiburg/Rennes.
Ich habe einige Andenken gekauft und viele Fotos gemacht.	I bought some souvenirs and took a lot of photos.
Das Essen schmeckt mir sehr gut.	I like the food a lot.
Ich esse gern Pizza/Nudeln/ Hähnchen mit Pommes.	I like pizza/noodles/chicken and chips.
Das Eis ist lecker.	The ice cream is delicious.
Wir bekommen frische Brötchen zum Frühstück.	We get fresh rolls for breakfast.
Das Essen schmeckt mir nicht.	I don't like the food.
Man isst viel Wurst hier.	They eat a lot of sausage/salami here.
Ich habe einen netten Jungen/ein nettes Mädchen kennen gelernt.	I've got to know a nice boy/girl.
Wir gehen heute Abend in die Disco.	We are going to the disco this evening.
Morgen fahren wir in die Berge.	We are going into the mountains tomorrow.
Am Wochenende möchten wir eine Radtour machen.	At the weekend we would like to go on a cycling tour.

Greetings and Good Wishes

Frohe Weihnachten!/ Fröhliche Weihnachten!	Happy Christmas!
Frohe Ostern!	Happy Easter!
Ein gutes neues Jahr!/Ein glückliches neues Jahr!	Happy New Year!

Ich gratuliere dir zum Geburtstag./Herzlichen Glückwunsch zum Geburtstag!	Happy Birthday!
Ich schenke dir ein kleines Buch über Irland.	I'm sending you a little book about Ireland as a present.
Hoffentlich gefällt es dir.	I hope you like it.
Gute Reise!	Have a good trip!
Schönes Wochenende!	Have a nice weekend!
Schöne Ferien!	Enjoy your holidays!
Komm gut nach Hause!	Come home safely!
Viel Spaß!	Have fun!/Enjoy yourself!
Mach's gut!	Bye! Take care!
Viel Glück!	Good luck!
Viel Erfolg!	I wish you every success!
Gute Besserung!	Get well soon!
Ich wünsche dir alles Gute./ Alles Gute!	I wish you all the best./ All the best!

Invitations, Thanks, Acceptances, Regrets

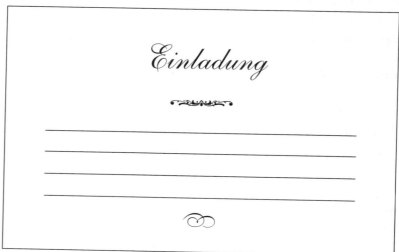

Du bist zu meiner Geburtstagsparty eingeladen.	You are invited to my birthday party.
Ich lade dich zu einer Weihnachtsparty ein.	I am inviting you to a Christmas party.
Möchtest du uns zu Ostern besuchen?	Would you like to visit us at Easter?
Möchtest du im Sommer drei Wochen bei uns verbringen?	Would you like to spend three weeks with us in the summer?
Frag deine Eltern!	Ask your parents.
Meine Schwester möchte dich zu ihrer Hochzeit am 25. August einladen.	My sister would like to invite you to her wedding on 25 August.
Danke/Schönen Dank für die Einladung.	Thank you for the invitation.
Ich komme gerne.	I'd love to come.
Ich freue mich darauf.	I'm looking forward to it.
Ich kann deine Einladung leider nicht annehmen.	Unfortunately, I can't accept your invitation.
Es tut mir leid, dass ich nicht kommen kann.	I'm sorry I can't come.
Schade, dass ich nicht kommen kann.	Pity I can't come.
Wir haben nämlich einen Familienurlaub geplant.	We have actually planned a family holiday.
Ich mache Prüfungen. Ich muss viel lernen.	I am doing exams. I have to do a lot of study.

Message

Ihre Schwester hat vor kurzem angerufen.	Your sister phoned a short while ago.
Deine Freundin Ute hat um 10 Uhr angerufen.	Your friend Ute phoned at 10 o'clock.
Ihre Nachbarin, Frau Weber, hat um 4.30 Uhr angerufen.	Your neighbour, Mrs Weber, phoned at 4.30.
Der Elektriker, Herr Geesing, ist um 12 Uhr vorbeigekommen.	The electrician, Mr Geesing, called round at 12 o'clock.
Peter/Sabine ist heute Nachmittag vorbeigekommen.	Peter/Sabine called round this afternoon.

Sie kommt heute Nachmittag am Hauptbahnhof an.	She is arriving this afternoon at the main station.
Können Sie sie um 17.15 Uhr abholen?	Can you pick her up at 17.15?
Sie hat viel Gepäck.	She has a lot of luggage.
Er kommt um halb vier vorbei.	He is calling round at half past three.
Sie will Sie morgen um 5 Uhr treffen, wenn das Ihnen passt.	She wants to meet you tomorrow at 5 o'clock if that suits you.
Er kommt morgen wieder.	He is coming back tomorrow.
Sie ruft heute Abend zurück.	She will phone back this evening.
Du sollst sie zurückrufen.	You should call her back.
Peter kann dich am Montag leider nicht treffen.	Unfortunately, Peter can't meet you on Monday.
Er hat nämlich einen Termin.	He actually has an appointment.
Wie wäre es mit Dienstag?	How about Tuesday?
Sabine kann heute Abend nicht mit ins Kino gehen.	Sabine can't go to the cinema with you this evening.
Ihr Vater musste ins Krankenhaus und sie will ihn besuchen.	Her father had to go into hospital and she wants to visit him.

Explaining Absence

Ich gehe jetzt zur Post, um Briefmarken zu kaufen.	I am going to the post office to buy stamps.
Ich muss Briefe einwerfen.	I have to post letters.
Ich treffe Martin in der Stadt.	I am meeting Martin in town.
Wir gehen ins Schwimmbad.	We are going to the swimming pool.
Maria ist vorbeigekommen. Wir gehen spazieren.	Maria called round. We are going for a walk.
Ich komme um 7 Uhr zum Abendessen zurück.	I will come back at 7 o'clock for dinner.
Ich bin in einer Stunde wieder da.	I'll be back in an hour.
Ich komme später zurück.	I'll come back later.
Ich werde bis 9 Uhr wieder da sein.	I'll be back by 9 o'clock.

Notice Board

Verloren   *Lost*

Mein Hund ging verloren. Hat jemand ihn gesehen?
My dog is lost. Has anybody seen him?

Er ist klein und schwarz und trägt ein Halsband mit dem Namen Arno.
He is small and black and is wearing a collar with the name Arno.

Belohnung für den Finder.
Reward for the finder.

Ich habe mein Deutschheft verloren. Hat jemand es gefunden?
I've lost my German copy. Has anyone found it?

Gefunden   *Found*

Ich habe heute neben dem Tennisplatz eine Brille gefunden.
I found a pair of glasses beside the tennis court today.

Sie hat einen blauen Rahmen.
It has a blue frame.

Ruf mich unter der Nummer . . . an!
Ring me at . . . .

Wer hat Interesse an einer Radtour?
Who is interested in a cycling tour?

Wer möchte mitkommen?
Who would like to come along?

Habt ihr Interesse an Gitarrestunden?	Are you interested in guitar lessons?
Wer braucht Nachhilfe?	Who needs grinds?
Sie können mich abends erreichen.	You can reach me in the evenings.
Ich wohne bei Familie Schmidt, Mozartstr. 10.	I am staying with the Schmidt family, 10 Mozartstr.
Man findet mich in der Jugendherberge.	I am at the youth hostel.

Request to a Penpal

Ich mache ein Projekt über das deutsche Schulsystem.	I am doing a project on the German school system.
Ich mache ein Projekt über österreichische Musiker.	I am doing a project on Austrian musicians.
Hilfe!	Help!
Kannst du mir helfen?	Can you help me?
Kannst du deine Schule und einen typischen Schultag beschreiben?	Can you describe your school and a typical school day?
Könntest du mir bitte Informationen schicken?	Could you please send me information?
Ich brauche Bilder, Broschüren und so weiter.	I need pictures, brochures and so on.
Ich bin gut nach Hause gekommen.	I arrived home safely.
Leider kann ich meinen Fotoapparat/meine Uhr/mein Portemonnaie nicht finden.	Unfortunately, I can't find my camera/my watch/my purse.
Ich glaube, ich habe ihn/sie/es im Zimmer liegen lassen.	I think I left it behind in the room.
Kannst du ihn/sie/es mir nachschicken?	Can you send it on to me?
Meine Freundin sucht eine Brieffreundin aus Deutschland/aus der Schweiz.	My friend is looking for a penpal from Germany/from Switzerland.

Kannst du jemanden für sie finden?	Can you find someone for her?
Sie ist dreizehn Jahre alt und sehr sportlich.	She is thirteen and very sporty.

Formal Requests

Sehr geehrte Damen und Herren,	Dear Sir or Madam,

When writing to a youth hostel:

Lieber Herbergsvater,	Dear Warden, (m.)
Liebe Herbergsmutter,	Dear Warden, (f.)
Liebe Herbergseltern,	Dear Wardens, (pl.)

Mit freundlichen Grüßen	Yours sincerely
Ihr (m.)	Yours
Ihre (f.)	

Verkehrsamt	*Tourist office*
Könnten Sie mir/uns Informationen über die Stadt schicken?	Could you send me/us information about the town?

Ich suche eine Unterkunft.	I'm looking for accommodation.
Bitte schicken Sie mir Broschüren und eine Liste von Hotels in der Umgebung.	Please send me brochures and a list of hotels in the area.
Ich wäre Ihnen sehr dankbar, wenn Sie mir Broschüren und einen Stadtplan schicken könnten.	I would be very grateful if you could send me brochures and a map of the town.
Ich hätte gern Informationen über die Sehenswürdigkeiten.	I would like information about the tourist sites.
Was gibt es in der Gegend zu tun und zu sehen?	What is there to do and to see in the area?
Ich danke Ihnen im Voraus für Ihre Hilfe.	Thank you in advance for your help.

Campingurlaub

Camping holiday

Ich möchte im Juni einen Campingurlaub in Deutschland machen.	I would like to go on a camping holiday in Germany in June.
Ich habe vor, mit zwei Freunden zu zelten.	I intend to go camping with two friends.
Wir haben unseren eigenen Wohnwagen.	We have our own caravan.
Wir haben vor, vom 3. bis zum 12. Juni auf Ihrem Campingplatz zu bleiben.	We intend to stay in your campsite from 3 to 12 June.
Haben Sie Platz für ein Zelt/ einen Wohnwagen?	Have you space for a tent/a caravan?
Welche Einrichtungen haben Sie?	What facilities have you?
Kann man dort Fahrräder mieten?	Can we hire bicycles there?
Gibt es ein Lebensmittel- geschäft/einen Fernsehraum auf dem Campingplatz?	Is there a grocery store/a TV room on the campsite?

Jugendherberge

Youth hostel

Wir haben vor, im Sommer nach Österreich zu fahren.	We intend to go to Austria in the summer.
Wir sind vier Mädchen/Jungen.	We are four girls/boys.
Haben Sie vom 4. bis zum 8. August Platz frei?	Have you vacancies from 4 to 8 August?
Was kostet eine Übernachtung mit Frühstück?	How much does one night with breakfast cost?
Welche Mahlzeiten gibt es?	What meals are there?
Darf man selbst kochen?	May we cook for ourselves?
Kann man Bettwäsche leihen oder muss man Schlafsäcke mitbringen?	Can we hire bed linen or do we have to bring sleeping bags?
Wir freuen uns auf Ihre Antwort.	We are looking forward to your answer.

Hotel

Hotel

Meine Familie möchte vom 12. bis zum 15. Juli in Ihrem Hotel bleiben.	My family would like to stay in your hotel from 12 to 15 July.
Wir sind zwei Erwachsene und drei Kinder.	We are two adults and three children.
Wir möchten zwei Doppelzimmer mit Bad und Dusche und ein Einzelzimmer mit Dusche.	We would like two double rooms with bath and shower and one single room with shower.
Könnten Sie bitte möglichst bald die Reservierung bestätigen?	Could you please confirm the reservation as soon as possible?

PAST EXAM QUESTIONS

Here are some samples from previous exam papers.

2004: Postcard

You are with your family on holiday and write a postcard to your **German** penpal. Include the following details:

- Say where you are and how long you are staying.
- Describe the bad weather.
- Say how you find the food.
- Mention two things you did yesterday.

(Write approximately **25–30** words.)

Sample answer (two versions):

Liebe Bettina,

Grüße aus Italien. Wir machen einen Familienurlaub hier. Wir bleiben zwei Wochen. Das Wetter ist leider nicht gut. Es gibt Gewitter und es regnet viel. Das italienische Essen ist lecker. Gestern haben wir einen Dom besichtigt und ich habe einige Andenken gekauft.
Deine
Rose

Lieber Thomas,
ich bin für eine Woche mit meiner Familie hier in Dingle. Das Wetter ist furchtbar. Es ist kalt und windig. Es gibt viele Fischrestaurants hier und ich esse gern Fisch. Gestern sind wir ins Hallenbad gegangen und später haben wir im Ferienhaus ferngesehen.
Dein
Brendan

2003: Short Note

You are staying with your penpal Uli. One evening, while his parents are out, Uli gets sick. Leave a note for Uli's parents saying:

- Uli is sick in bed.
- Mention two of his symptoms.
- You have gone to the pharmacy.
- You'll be back in half an hour.

(Write approximately **25–30** words.)

Sample answer (two versions):

Uli ist im Bett. Er fühlt sich nicht wohl.

Er hat Bauchschmerzen und Kopfschmerzen.

Ich gehe zur Apotheke.

Ich komme in einer halben Stunde zurück. Kevin.

Uli ist krank und er ist ins Bett gegangen. Er hat Halsschmerzen und Fieber. Ich gehe jetzt zur Apotheke und bin in einer halben Stunde wieder da. Aisling.

2002: Short Note for Notice Board

You are spending three months on an exchange programme in Germany. You would like to give grinds (Nachhilfe) in English to get some extra pocket money. Write a short note for the school notice board saying:

- who you are and where you are from
- that you give grinds in English
- how much it costs per hour
- you are in room 23 on the second floor.

(Write approximately **25–30** words.)

Sample answer (two versions):

> Ich heiße Mary und komme aus Irland. Ich mache einen Schüleraustausch. Ich gebe Nachhilfe in Englisch. Eine Stunde kostet 20€. Ich bin in Zimmer 23 im zweiten Stock.

> Wer hat Interesse an Nachhilfe in Englisch? Ich gebe Nachhilfestunden (20€ pro Stunde). Ich komme aus Irland und heiße Liam. Du findest mich in Zimmer 23 im zweiten Stock.

2002: Postcard

You are doing a project on 'food in Switzerland'. You write to your penfriend asking him/her to send you some material for it. Write a postcard saying:

- you are doing a project on food in Switzerland
- when you must have it finished
- what materials you need
- thanks for his/her help.

(Write approximately **25–30** words.)

Sample answer (two versions):

> Liebe Dani,
> ich mache ein Projekt über das Essen in der Schweiz. Ich muss in zwei Wochen fertig sein. Ich brauche Broschüren, Speisekarten und Rezepte. Vielen Dank im Voraus für deine Hilfe.
> Deine
> Eleanor

```
Lieber Erik,
Wie geht's? Unsere Klasse macht ein Projekt
über die Schweiz und ich muss über das Essen
schreiben. Kannst du mir helfen? Ich muss bis
Ende Mai fertig sein. Ich möchte Bilder,
Broschüren und vielleicht ein Kochbuch.
Danke für deine Hilfe.
            Dein
            Henry
```

1999: Postcard to a Youth Hostel

Write a postcard to the warden of the youth hostel at the given address in which you:

- state that you and two friends are planning to visit Germany in the summer (give dates);
- enquire if there is space in the youth hostel at that time;
- ask how much an overnight stay with breakfast costs;
- ask if it is possible to hire bikes.

(Write approximately **25–35** words.)

Sample answer:

```
Lieber Herbergsvater,
ich fahre im Sommer mit zwei
Freunden nach Deutschland. Wir
kommen am 5. August an und bleiben      An den Herbergsvater
bis zum 12. August. Haben Sie zu
diesem Zeitpunkt Platz frei? Was         DJH
kostet eine Übernachtung mit
Frühstück? Kann man Fahrräder            Bachstraße 3
mieten?
            Mit freundlichen Grüßen      D-69115 Heidelberg
            Ihre Susan Moloney
```

1998: Short Note (Phone message)

You are at your penpal's house in Vienna. The phone rings when **everyone else is out**, so you answer and **take a message** from your penpal's friend. Write down in German the following points:

- Karen phoned at 3.30 p.m.
- She can't go to the concert tomorrow evening.
- She has a test on Friday and has a lot of homework.
- She'll phone back later.

(Write approximately **25–35** words.)

Sample answer:

> Deine Freundin Karen hat heute Nachmittag um halb vier angerufen. Sie kann morgen Abend nicht ins Konzert gehen. Sie hat am Freitag eine Klassenarbeit und hat viele Hausaufgaben. Sie ruft später zurück.
> Patricia

1995: Short Note to the 'Verkehrsamt'

Your family is thinking about going to Koblenz on holiday. Write a short note to the Verkehrsamt (tourist office) there and include the following:

- ask if they could send you a brochure and a town map of Koblenz
- ask what there is to do and see in the area
- ask for a price list of hotels
- say thank-you for the help.

(Write approximately **25–35** words.)

12 Barrack Street,
Dublin 4,
Ireland

Verkehrsamt
Lahnstr. 52
56077 Koblenz

Sehr geehrte Damen und Herren,

_____

_____

_____

Mit freundlichen Grüßen
Ihr(e) . . . .

Sample answer:

12 Barrack Street,
Dublin 4,
Ireland

Verkehrsamt
Lahnstr. 52
56077 Koblenz

Sehr geehrte Damen und Herren,

Meine Familie würde gern in Koblenz Urlaub machen. Könnten Sie uns bitte eine Broschüre und einen Stadtplan schicken? Was gibt es in der Gegend zu tun und zu sehen? Wir möchten auch eine Preisliste von Hotels.

Danke im Voraus für Ihre Hilfe.

Mit freundlichen Grüßen
Ihr(e) . . . .

4. PAST EXAMINATION PAPER AND SOLUTIONS

Past Junior Certificate Examination Paper
German – Higher Level

9.30 to 12.00

Section I – Listening Comprehension

(140 marks)

Listen very carefully to the CD and to the instructions given on it.

A

You will hear <u>two extracts</u> from a CD made by German-speaking pupils. **Tanja and Theo introduce themselves**. Listen to them and fill in, <u>in English</u>, the details required below.

You will hear each extract <u>twice</u>. There will be a pause after each hearing.

	Extract (1)	Extract (2)
Name	**Tanja**	**Theo**
Description of appearance (**Three** details)		
Birthday		
Did what on her/his birthday		
Presents received (Name **two**)		
Going **with whom** on holidays		
Going **where** on holidays		
Activities planned (Name **two**)		

B

You will hear <u>three</u> separate conversations. Listen carefully and answer the questions <u>in English</u>. You will hear each conversation <u>twice</u>. There will be a pause after each hearing.

1. (Getting directions)

(i) Where is the person looking for directions to?

_____

(ii) Describe the recommended route.

_____

_____

2. (At the dentist)

(i) Where is Susi's toothache located?

_____

(ii) What advice does the dentist give regarding brushing teeth? Give details.

_____

_____

(iii) What advice does the dentist give about eating?

_____

_____

3. (Fashion department)

(i) Describe **two** items that Laura admires.

_____

_____

(ii) *(a)* Which item does Laura want to buy? *(b)* How much does it cost?

(a) _____   *(b)* _____

(iii) How can Laura afford to buy it?

_____

_____

C

You will hear <u>three</u> separate items. Listen carefully and answer the questions <u>in English</u>. You will hear each item <u>twice</u>. There will be a pause after each hearing.

1. (Youth hostel)

(i) *(a)* Karl makes a booking in the youth hostel. For whom? Give details.

_____

(b) Why do they not need to hire bed-linen?

_____

(ii) *(a)* Where are the rooms located?   *(b)* What are the room numbers?

Girls *(a)* _____   *(b)* _____

Boys *(a)* _____   *(b)* _____

(iii) Why is the table-tennis room closed at the moment?

_____

2. (Festival advertisement)

(i) Name **four** of the attractions listed in the advertisement for the festival.

_____

_____

(ii) *(a)* For whom is the festival intended?

_____

(b) **Where** does the festival take place? Give details.

_____

(iii) Complete *(a)* the telephone number and *(b)* the e-mail address mentioned.

(a) **4000–** _____   *(b)* **www.** _____

3. (Shopping list)

Arne needs some vegetables for his cookery class. Write down, **in English**, what he needs for the recipe.

_____

EXAMPLE:

500 g	Potatoes
200 g	
A packet of	
4	
150 g	
150 g	

D

You will hear each of two conversations <u>three times</u>, the second time with pauses. Listen carefully and answer the questions in <u>English</u>.

1. (Andi and Tina want to go to the concert)

(i) *(a)* **When** is the concert?

_____

(b) How much do the tickets cost?

_____

(ii) *(a)* Why are Tina's parents upset with her?

_____

_____

(b) Which subjects does Andi find difficult and why?

_____

_____

(iii) What plan do they have to improve Tina's chances of getting to the concert? Give details.

_____

_____

2. (At School)

(i) *(a)* What news did Michael hear?   *(b)* Why does he find it hard to believe?

(a) _____

(b) _____

_____

(ii) *(a)* What suggestions does Sabine make for a present?

_____

(b) What do they eventually decide to buy?

_____

(iii) What do they decide to do on *(a)* Friday and *(b)* Thursday?

(a) Friday _____

(b) Thursday _____

E

You will hear a conversation <u>three times</u>, the second time with pauses. Listen carefully and answer the questions <u>in English</u>.

(Interview with Sinead)

1. Why did Sinead come on a school exchange to Germany? Give details.

_____

_____

2. *(a)* Where is she staying during her exchange? Give details.

_____

_____

(b) How does she describe Ireland? Give details.

_____

_____

3. List the differences Sinead notices between the German school and school in Ireland.

_____

_____

4. What does Sinead miss about Ireland? Give details.

_____

_____

5. What does Sinead normally do in her free time at home? Give details.

_____

_____

Read the information carefully and then answer as instructed in each case.

A

1. You are in a German school for a few weeks and you have P.E. in the **sports hall** next class. Where do you go? **Rewrite** the chosen word.

SPORTPLATZ	TURNHALLE	GYMNASIUM	LABOR

_____

2. You are looking for the **departure** sign at the railway station. What sign do you look for? **Rewrite** the chosen word.

ABFAHRT	AUSGANG	ANKUNFT	ANFANG

_____

3. You want to tell your German exchange student that it will be **foggy** later tonight. Which word will you use? **Rewrite** the chosen word.

BEDECKT	NEBELIG	WOLKIG	TROCKEN

_____

B

Write the <u>number</u> of the **ADVERTISEMENT** beside the item, message or service it is advertising. **Beware of extra items!**

Number	
	Summer courses
	Windows & Doors
	Mountaineering
3	Coffee-table book
	Porcelain
	Painter/Decorator
	Travel agency
	Disco
	Rail exhibition
	Magazine

1

Alt
Meissner Porzellan
Verkaufsausstellung von Weltrang
Über 800 Exponate aus drei Jh.
Fr. 25. 3. - Mi. 30. 3.
Täglich 10.00 - 20.00 Uhr
DOLDER GRAND HOTEL
ZURICH

2

Gornergrat
SCHWEIZ
Revue Schweiz Suisse Svizzera Switzerland

Das Magazin für Reisen, Kultur und Natur

☐ 1 Probeexemplar gratis
☐ 1 Jahresabonnement für Fr. 69.–
(8 Ausgaben), zusätzl. 1 Ausgabe gratis

Name:

Strasse:

PLZ/Ort:

Coupon bitte einsenden an:
Revue SCHWEIZ, Postfach, 4501 Solothurn
Telefon 032 623 16 33, Fax 032 623 50 36

3

EIN BASLER PANORAMA

Peter Gartmann/Hans-Peter Platz

Ein Basler Panorama

Die Schönheit Basels in querformatigen Bildern aneinandergereiht – ergänzt mit einer Liebeserklärung an die Stadt am Rhein.

144 Seiten, 90 farbige Panoramabilder, gebunden
CHF 48.–

Erhältlich im Buchhandel, ,
BaZ am Barfi, BaZ Liestal,
BaZ Hochbergerstrasse 15,
Postfach, 4002 Basel
Telefon 061/639 13 15
Fax   061/639 13 43
E-Mail: order@baz.ch

4

5

6

7

C

Read through the advertisements, and answer the questions in <u>English</u>.

1.

CAMPUS AUSTRIA *Sprachschulen*

Unsere Institute bieten an:
- Kinder- und Jugendsprachkurse
- Deutschkurse für Erwachsene
- Deutsch für den Beruf
- Lehrerkurse
- Einzelstunden für Individuen.

SPASS UND SPORT
Ski fahren, Reiten, Tennis, Federball, Badeferien – toller Urlaub, super für Kontakte!

KULTURELLES & LANDESTYPISCHES
Österreichische Kultur erleben! Walzer-Tanzkurs in Wien, Salzburger Festspiele, Kultur-Spaziergang in Graz.

1. (i) Mention **four** courses or classes offered by **Campus Austria** language schools.

_____

_____

_____

(ii) List **four** sports mentioned.

_____

_____

(iii) Mention **two** cultural activities recommended.

_____

_____

2.

Egal, was Sie in Wien machen wollen: Mit der Wien-Karte kommen Sie überall hin. Die Wien-Karte gilt 72 Stunden für U-Bahn, Straßenbahn und Bus (ausgenommen Nightline Busse).

Bitte beachten Sie! Mit der Wien-Karte können Sie ein Kind bis zum 15. Lebensjahr (**Ausweis nötig!**) frei mitnehmen. *Und* Sie können viele Sehenswürdigkeiten zum halben Preis besuchen.

Erleben Sie Wien. Mit den Wiener Linien. Nähere Informationen erhalten Sie in Ihrem Hotel.

2. (i) Which types of transport can one use with the **Wien-Karte**?
(Paragraph 1)

_____

_____

(ii) Name **one** extra benefit of the **Wien-Karte.**
(Paragraph 2)

_____

_____

D

In each of the following three questions, indicate your answer by <u>writing the</u> <u>appropriate sentence on the line provided</u>.

(i) You cannot **find your copy**. What do you say to your teacher?
(a) Kann ich mein Heft haben?
(b) Ich kann mein Heft nicht finden.
(c) Ich habe mein Buch verloren.
(d) Ich finde meinen Kuli nicht.

_____

(ii) The teacher wants to know if the pupils have any **questions**. What does he/she say?
(a) Wie lautet die Antwort?
(b) Frag mal!
(c) Habt ihr Fragen?
(d) Beantworte die Frage!

_____

(iii) The teacher asks two pupils **to come and sit at the front of the class**. What does he/she say?
(a) Setzt euch hier vorne hin!
(b) Setz dich dahin!
(c) Bleibt da sitzen!
(d) Stell dich hinten an!

_____

E

Read through the following notices advertising **holiday jobs**. Then fill in the information required, **in English**, in the spaces provided. The required information from box **(1)** has been filled in as an example.

(1)
Gartenzentrum
Gesucht: Aushilfskraft für unser Gartenzentrum im Juli und August.
Arbeitszeiten: Montag-Freitag, 9 bis 17 Uhr.
Aufgaben: Rasen mähen, Blumen pflanzen und Kunden bedienen.
Stundenlohn: 7€
Information: Tim Lemanski,
                Gartenzentrum Lemanski.
                Tel: 0511–15430.

(2)
Tankstelle
30€ pro Tag. Wir suchen tüchtige Jugendliche zum Auto waschen, zum Tanken und um im Laden zu helfen. Vier Wochenenden im August.
Arbeitserfahrung nicht nötig. Bitte melde dich bei M. Kerz: Tel. 02104–548773.

(3)
Restaurant zum Ochsen
Gesucht: Engagierte Küchenhilfe für die Sommerferien, Donnerstag-Sonntag.
Aufgaben: Geschirr spülen/ abtrocknen, Gemüse und Kartoffeln schälen.
Stundenlohn: 6,50€
Kontakt: Frau Meinach,
Tel. 030–647791.

(4)
Tierheim Starnberg
Tierfreunde gesucht! Samstags und montags von Juni bis August suchen wir junge Leute, die mit Hunden spazieren gehen, Katzen und Kaninchen füttern und kranke Tiere zum Tierarzt bringen.
Bezahlung: Keine, aber 80 Tiere danken euch! Meldet euch bei Fabian:
Tel. 089–337281.

	Where	When	What duties	Pay	Contact whom
(1)	Garden centre	July–August Mon–Fri 9 am–5 pm	Mow lawns, plant flowers, serve customers.	€7 per hour	Tim Lemanksi at Lemanski's garden centre. Tel: 0511–15430
(2)					
(3)					
(4)					

Read through this article and answer the questions which follow <u>in English</u>.

Tattoos und Piercing – die neue Mode

Tattoos und Piercing sind die Mode-erscheinung des neuen Jahrhunderts: Tattoos auf dem Arm, dem Knöchel und dem Rücken. Piercings im Ohr, in der Nase, der Zunge oder im Bauchnabel sind populär.

Viele Jugendliche stellen ihren Eltern die gleiche Frage: „Darf ich ein Tattoo oder Piercing haben?" Die meisten Eltern antworten ohne zu zögern mit: „Nein". Und dann nutzt alles Bitten und Betteln nichts. Die Gründe sind klar, die Eltern sagen: „Das ist hässlich. Und auch gefährlich – du bekommst Narben.* Wenn du älter bist, findest du es garantiert nicht mehr schön!" Aber viele Jugendliche machen es trotzdem.

Dann das Problem Geld. Es ist teuer. Soll man Taschengeld sparen, jobben, auf Weihnachten warten? Auf dem Weg zum Piercing-Studio kommt dann manchmal doch Angst auf. Wird es weh tun? Wie muss ich es sauber halten? Was passiert, wenn ich eine Infektion bekomme? Was werden die Freunde denken?

Die meisten Freunde mögen Elodies Tattoo.

Wenn man auf dem Stuhl im Studio sitzt, ist es meistens zu spät. Kurz danach geht man aus dem Studio nach Hause, hat viel Geld ausgegeben und fühlt sich dennoch glücklich – aber auch etwas nervös.

Dann zeigt man stolz den neuen Körperschmuck. Die Reaktion der Eltern: „Mein Gott, das ist ja gefährlich! Du musst sofort zum Arzt. Das geht nur noch mit Laser weg." Die meisten Freunde finden den Körperschmuck schön. Sie bewundern ihn wie einen neuen Haarschnitt und wollen selber einen haben.

*Narben = scars

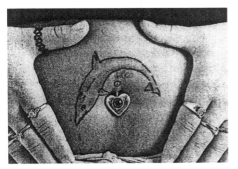

„Piercing ist so ähnlich wie das Tragen von Ohrringen", findet Deborah.

1. Tattoos and body-piercing are fashionable among young people. What, according to the article, are the most popular body parts for *(a)* tattoos and *(b)* body-piercing? **(Paragraph 1)**

(a) _____

(b) _____

2. Most parents object when their children ask if they can get a tattoo or a body-piercing. What arguments do parents use? **(Paragraph 2)**

_____

_____

_____

3. *(a)* How do young people pay for tattoos and body-piercing?
   (b) On the way to the tattoo and body-piercing studio young people often get nervous. What questions do they ask themselves? **(Paragraph 3)**

(a) _____

_____

(b) _____

_____

4. How do they usually feel after the procedure? **(Paragraph 4)**

_____

_____

5. How do *(a)* parents and *(b)* friends usually react to the new body decoration? Give details. **(Paragraph 5)**

(a) Parents _____

_____

_____

(b) Friends _____

_____

_____

G

Answer <u>in English</u> the questions which follow the passage.

Oma findet Fußballspielen gut

In der Schule war Kalle in der dritten Klasse und nicht in allen Fächern gut. Er machte auch nicht immer die Hausaufgaben. Aber die meisten in seiner Klasse hatten ihn gern. Er hatte tolle Ideen für Spiele, er erzählte lustige Witze und war vor allem ein sehr guter Fußballspieler.

Sein Freund Peter hatte die Idee, dass die dritte Klasse ein Fußballspiel gegen die vierte Klasse organisieren sollte. Am ersten Tag trainierten sie in den Pausen. Dann sagten die Lehrer, sie sollten **5** sich nachmittags auf dem Sportplatz treffen. Die Lehrer wollten beim Training helfen. Kalle fand das prima.

Kalle wohnte bei seiner Oma. Am Wochenende erzählte er ihr von dem geplanten Fußballspiel. Aber seine Oma war dagegen. „Du könntest dir das Bein brechen! Du könntest dich am Kopf verletzen! Also, das geht nicht, Kalle." Kalle war sehr enttäuscht. „Bitte, lass mich doch gehen: Am Donnerstag **10** ist das erste Training. Es ist doch gesund, in der frischen Luft Fußball zu spielen. Viel besser als Fernseh gucken. Alle meine Freunde spielen mit!" Oma konnte nicht hart bleiben. Endlich sagte sie: „Ja". Sie fragte Kalle, auf welchem Sportplatz sie spielen wollten. „Gar nicht so weit von hier", antwortete Kalle. „Auf dem Grün-Weiß-Platz neben dem Eisstadion." So ging Kalle am Donnerstag zum Training. **15**

Ein junger Lehrer war schon da. Er zeigte den Schülern: Wie man Bälle stoppt, mit der Brust oder mit dem Fuß, wie man mit der Seite oder der Spitze des Fußes kickt. Kalle lernte auch, wie man einen Kopfball schießt. Das konnte Kalle besser als die anderen.

Dann kam endlich der große Tag. Mitten im Spiel sah Kalle plötzlich seine Oma am Rande des Fußballplatzes. Sie winkte ihm zu, aber er schämte sich und sah weg. Und dann begann Oma auch **20** noch zu schreien. „Schneller, Kalle! Lass dir den Ball nicht wegnehmen!" rief sie. Ein Lehrer ging zu ihr hin, und sie redeten ein paar Minuten lang. Kalle sah die beiden. Der Lehrer lachte laut. Oma blieb bis zum Ende. Von da an gab es keine Probleme, wenn Kalle zum Training gehen wollte.

---

1. What information is given in the first paragraph about Kalle? Mention **four** details.

(Lines 1–3)

_____

_____

_____

_____

2. *(a)* What was Peter's idea?   **(Lines 4–5)**
   (b) What did the teachers suggest?   **(Lines 5–6)**

(a) _____

_____

(b) _____

_____

_____

3. (a) Kalle's grandmother was against the idea at first. Why?   **(Lines 9–10)**

  (b) What arguments did Kalle use to persuade his grandmother to let him go? List **two.**   **(Lines 10–12)**

(a) _____

_____

(b) _____

_____

_____

4. What techniques did the players learn from the young teacher? Give details.

(Lines 16–18)

_____

_____

5. (a) How did Kalle react when he saw his grandmother at the sidelines?

(Lines 19–20)

  (b) What did Kalle's grandmother shout from the sidelines? **(Lines 20–21)**

(a) _____

(b) _____

_____

Section III – Written Expression

(80 marks)

The **lined pages** which follow the questions are to be used for answering (**A**) and (**B**).

A

LETTER

You have received a letter from your Swiss exchange partner. Write a letter in reply, answering all the questions (which have been numbered for you) in some detail. (**120 words minimum**)

Luzern, den 7. Juni 2003

Liebe/r .... ,
ich habe lange nichts mehr von dir gehört und habe mir gedacht, ich schreibe dir doch mal wieder. Ich hätte dir am liebsten eine E-Mail geschickt, weiß aber deine E-Mail Adresse nicht. Ich verbringe im Moment viel Zeit an meinem Computer – mindestens 2 Stunden am Tag. Das ist mein Hobby. (**1**) Was machst du denn gerne in deiner Freizeit? Wie oft und wo machst du das?

Du hast mir geschrieben, dass du in einem Haus wohnst. (**2**) Kannst du dein Haus beschreiben? Wie viele Zimmer habt ihr? Habt ihr einen Garten? Wir wohnen in einem Wohnblock in der Stadtmitte von Luzern. Die Wohnung ist recht klein, aber ich habe mein eigenes Zimmer. Ich lege dir ein paar Fotos bei. Leider sind Haustiere nicht erlaubt. Du hast neulich geschrieben, ihr wolltet ein Haustier kaufen. (**3**) Was für ein Tier ist das? Kannst du es mir beschreiben? Wie teuer war es?

Schreib mir von dem Sprachkurs, den du gemacht hast. (**4**) Wann und wo war das genau? Was habt ihr alles im Kurs gemacht?

Ich möchte deiner Familie dieses Jahr etwas zu Weihnachten aus der Schweiz schicken. Ich weiß aber nicht, was. (**5**) Was denkst du? Kannst du mir ein paar Tipps geben? Bitte schreib diesmal schneller zurück!

Tschüss,
     dein(e)
     Kai

P.S. Meine E-Mail Adresse ist: k.beil@freenet.ch

_____

_____

_____

_____

_____

_____

_____

_____

_____

_____

_____

B

SHORT NOTE

You are staying with your penpal Uli. One evening, while his parents are out, Uli gets sick. Leave a note for Uli's parents saying:

- Uli is sick and in bed.
- Mention two of his symptoms.
- You have gone to the pharmacy.
- You'll be back in half an hour.

(Write approximately **25–30** words)

_____

_____

_____

_____

Solutions and Marks

Stroke [/] indicates alternatives, any one of which is enough. Round brackets ( ) enclose information which is correct but not essential for marks.

Section I – Listening Comprehension

(140 marks)

A   (24 marks)

(12 x 2)

Tanja	Theo
Any three: Long/brown hair Blue eyes 1.60 (m) (tall) (Wears) glasses	*Any three:* Short/black hair Grey eyes 1.80 (m) tall (for age) (Very) slim/thin
9 June/last week	23 March
Party (with 10 friends) Barbecue Danced (a lot)	Went to Paris Went to Eurodisney/Disney(land) Photo with Mickey Mouse
Any two: Watch/clock Earrings Book(s) Ski jacket	*Any two:* Photo with Mickey Mouse CDs Runners/gym shoes Computer game(s)
Parents and sister	Youth club
Austria	Denmark
Any two: Skiing Ice-skating Walking (in snow)	*Any two:* Camping Swimming Sailing Windsurfing

B (25 marks)

1. (Getting directions) *(6 marks)*
    (i) Open-air/outdoor swimming pool.
    (ii) Straight on, first street right, past the church, as far as/to/by the river.

2. (At the dentist) *(8 marks)*
    (i) Bottom/Lower left.
    (ii) (Brush teeth) after every meal/after breakfast, lunch and dinner, for (at least) 3 minutes.
    (iii) Eat fewer sweets/sweet things/less confectionery/chocolate, not too many sweets, etc.

3. (Fashion department) *(11 marks)*
    (i) *Any two*: Short/red mini-skirt, white blouse/shirt, black/leather jacket.
    (ii) (a) Mini/skirt. (b) 79 (euro).
    (iii) Has got €100 from/was given €100 by aunt (Elisabeth).

C (31 marks)

1. (Youth hostel) *(9 marks)*
    (i) (a) 2 girls and 3 boys/5 people. (b) They have sleeping bags.
    (ii) (a) *Girls:* Ground floor, *boys:* 2nd floor. (b) *Girls:* (Room) 8, *boys:* (Room) 25.
    (iii) Window (is) broken.

2. (Festival advertisement) *(12 marks)*
    (i) *Any four:* Sport, games/play, drama/theatre, dancing, music, painting.
    (ii) (a) 6–12-year-olds. (b) Park in town/city/Vienna.
    (iii) (a) 84400. (b) fest.at

3. (Shopping list) *(10 marks)*
Tomatoes, spinach, onions, mushrooms, cheese.

D (32 marks)

1. (Andi and Tina want to go to the concert) *(18 marks)*
    (i) (a) September. (b) 60 (euro).
    (ii) (a) She failed/got an E/5 in/has bad marks/grades/results in maths.
        (b) English and Spanish. Verbs (confuse him), new words/vocabulary, grammar.
    (iii) Andi will help with maths homework.

2. (At school)   (14 marks)
    (i) (a) (Class) teacher/Mr Brandt/Herr Brandt has 50th birthday on Friday.
         (b) He looks younger/does not look so old.
    (ii) (a) (A bottle of) wine, a tie. (b) Book about Norway.
    (iii) (a) (Have a) party during history/in class/in school/in the morning.
         (b) (All) bring in/collect/get 5 euro.

E   (28 marks)

(Interview with Sinéad)
1. To improve/learn more German/the language, to get to know/learn more about Germany, meet young people.
2. (a) With a family, in the town/city (centre), in Bremen (b) Green/Emerald Isle, fields, meadows, rivers, lakes, the countryside/nature/natural landscape, it rains often/a lot.
3. School begins at 8 (a.m.) (in Germany), don't wear a uniform (in Germany), school over/finished at 1.30 (p.m.) (in Germany).
4. Her family, her little/younger brother, Ringo/her dog, her friends in (the) band.
5. Plays traditional/Irish music on the accordion/in a band.

Section II – Reading Comprehension

(100 marks)

A   (3 marks)

1. Turnhalle 2. Abfahrt 3. nebelig

B   (12 marks)

Number

6	Summer courses
7	Windows and doors
	Mountaineering
3	Coffee-table book
1	Porcelain
	Painter/Decorator
5	Travel agency
4	Disco
	Rail exhibition
2	Magazine

C   **(16 marks)**

1.   *(12 marks)*

   (i) *Any four:* (Courses for) children/young people, adults, career/profession(al), job, teachers/teaching, individuals/one to one.

  (ii) *Any four:* Skiing, riding, tennis, badminton, swimming/bathing.

 (iii) *Any two:* Waltzing/dancing (classes) in Vienna, festival(s) in Salzburg, (cultural) walk in Graz.

2.   *(4 marks)*

   (i) Underground/subway, tram, bus (except nightlink bus).

  (ii) *Any one:* You can take a/one child up to age 15 (for free), you can visit lots of (tourist) sights/sites for half price.

D   **(6 marks)**

   (i) (b) Ich kann mein Heft nicht finden.

  (ii) (c) Habt ihr Fragen?

 (iii) (a) Setzt euch hier vorne hin!

E   **(21 marks)**

(7 x 3)

1. [Example]

2. Filling/petrol/service station/garage. (4) weekends/at the weekend in August. Wash cars, fill petrol, help in shop. €30 per day. M. Kerz, Tel: 02104–548773.

3. Restaurant. Summer (holidays), Thursday–Sunday. Wash up/wash dishes, dry (up), peel/pare vegetables/potatoes. €6.50 per hour. Ms/Frau Meinach, Tel: 030–647791.

4. Animal home/shelter/sanctuary/rescue centre. Saturdays and Mondays, June–August. Walk dogs, feed cats/rabbits, (bring/take) sick animals to the vet. None/voluntary. Fabian, Tel: 089–337281.

F   **(20 marks)**

1. (a) Arm, ankle, back. (b) Ear, nose, tongue, belly-button/navel.

2. (They are) ugly/horrible, dangerous, you get scar(s), when you're older you won't think it's nice any more/you'll regret it.

3. (a) Save pocket money, work/part-time job, (wait for) Christmas.
   (b) Will it hurt? How do I keep it clean? What happens if I get an infection?/ Will it get infected? What will friends think?

4. Happy, nervous.

---

5. (a) (They say) 'My God, that is dangerous. You must go straight to the doctor. That can only be removed by laser.'
   (b) Most think it's beautiful/lovely/pretty/nice/they like it. They admire it like a new haircut. They want one.

<h1 style="text-align:center">G</h1>

(22 marks)

1. *Any four*: In 3rd class, not good at all/some subjects, didn't (always) do his homework, most (people) in his class liked him, had great ideas for games, told (funny) jokes/is funny, a (very) good football player.
2. (a) 3rd class/his class should have a football match/game against/with 4th class.
   (b) To meet in the afternoon at the sports ground/sports field/pitch to help with the training/football/to train/coach them.
3. (a) He could break his leg, he could injure/hurt his head.
   (b) *Any two*: It's healthy to play football in the fresh air, (much) better than watching TV, (all) his friends are playing/will be there.
4. How to stop the ball with the chest/foot, how to kick with the side/tip of the foot, how to head the ball.
5. (a) He was ashamed/embarrassed, he looked away.
   (b) Faster, Kalle! Don't let them get the ball (off you!)/don't lose possession (of the ball).

Section III – Written Expression

(80 marks)

A (Letter)   **(50 marks)**
   Content   *(30 marks)*
   Expression   *(20 marks)*
   (see sample letters on pp. 134 and 135)

B (Short Note)   **(30 marks)**
   Content   *(16 marks)*
   Expression   *(14 marks)*
   (see sample notes on p. 151)

Junior Certificate Examination, 2004

German – Higher Level

9.30 to 12.00

Section I – Listening Comprehension
(140 marks)

Listen very carefully to the recording and to the instructions given on it.

A

You will hear <u>two extracts</u> from a recording made by German-speaking pupils. **Claus und Maria talk about themselves**. Listen to them and fill in, <u>in English</u>, the details required below.

You will hear each extract <u>three times</u>. There will be a pause after each hearing.

Name	Claus	Maria
Birthday		
Favourite type of TV programme		
Type of school attended		
Favourite teacher		
Two reasons why this is the case		
Lives in what city?		
What is the city famous for? (**Two** details)		
Countries mentioned		

Extract (1) — Claus   Extract (2) — Maria

B

You will hear <u>three</u> separate conversations. Listen carefully and answer the questions <u>in English</u>. You will hear each conversation <u>twice</u>. There will be a pause after each hearing.

1. (Getting directions)

    (i) Where does the man want to go?

    _____

    (ii) What directions are given?

    _____

    _____

2. (At the lost property office)

    (i) When and exactly **where** does the lady think she left her bag? Give details.

    _____

    _____

    (ii) Describe the bag.

    _____

    _____

    (iii) *(a)* What was in her bag?   *(b)* What problem does this cause her?

    (a) _____

    (b) _____

    (iv) Complete the mobile phone number given.

    0179_____

3. (At the shopping centre)

    (i) Why is Susi going shopping?

    _____

    (ii) What are her father's hobbies?

    _____

    _____

    (iii) Describe the item she buys, including its price.

    _____

    _____

C

You will hear <u>three</u> separate items. Listen carefully and answer the questions <u>in</u> <u>English</u>. You will hear each item <u>twice</u>. There will be a pause after each hearing.

1. **(Holiday home for rent)**

   (i) Where is the house located?

   _____

   (ii) What details are given about the house?

   _____

   _____

   _____

   (iii) On what dates will Herr Gehring rent the house?

   _____

2. **(Department store announcement)**

   (i) What is on offer for €90? Give details.

   _____

   (ii) What is on special offer in the ladies' department? Give details.

   _____

   (iii) What is the closing time on Saturdays for this department store?

   _____

3. **(Recipe)**

Thomas wants to prepare a special dessert for the evening meal. Write down, **in English**, the ingredients needed.

Example: 250 g   **flour**
            3   _____
            ¼ litre _____
            2 tblsp. _____
            100 g   _____
            4   _____

D

You will hear each of two conversations <u>three times</u>, the second time with pauses. Listen carefully and answer the questions in <u>English</u>.

1. (Gone missing)

    (i) *(a)* What has Martina lost? *(b)* Where has she been looking for it? Give details.

        (a) _____

        (b) _____

              _____

    (ii) *(a)* How long has she been minding it?

              _____

        (b) When is Mario due to return?

              _____

    (iii) What does Tim suggest they do after the search? Give details.

              _____

              _____

2. (Planning the weekend)

    (i) Why is Sebastian not feeling well today? Give details.

              _____

              _____

              _____

    (ii) Why can he not go out with Maria before Saturday? Give details.

              _____

              _____

    (iii) What do they plan to do at the weekend? Give details.

              _____

              _____

              _____

    (iv) How much does the ticket cost?

              _____

E

You will hear a conversation <u>three times</u>, the second time with pauses. Listen carefully and answer the questions <u>in English</u>.

(Great news)

1. Why was Katrin not in school today?

_____

_____

2. Describe Katrin's sister. Give details.

_____

_____

3. What jobs must Katrin do before her mother comes home?

_____

_____

4. What present has Katrin bought for her sister?

_____

5. *(a)* What must Katrin ask her father to do this evening?

_____

_____

(b) Bernhard tells Katrin what homework was given. What homework must she do?

_____

_____

_____

Section II – Reading Comprehension

(100 marks)

Read the information carefully and then answer as instructed in each case.

A

1. You are in a supermarket and are looking for the **groceries** section. Where would you go? **Rewrite** the chosen word.

| GETRÄNKE | LEBENSMITTEL | SCHNELLIMBISS | SPEISEWAGEN |

2. You have witnessed an accident and would like to ring the **emergency number**. Which would you look for? **Rewrite** the chosen word.

| UNFALL | NOTAUSGANG | NOTRUF | FERNSPRECHER |

3. You have a runny nose and are looking for a **tissue**. What would you ask for? **Rewrite** the chosen word.

| TASCHENTUCH | HUSTEN | SCHNUPFEN | HANDTUCH |

B

Write the <u>number</u> of the **ADVERTISEMENT** beside the item, message or service it is advertising. **Beware of extra items.**

Number	
	Jeweller
	Holiday catalogue
4	Conservatories
	Florist
	Weightwatchers' club
	Pet supplies
	Camping shop
	Blood bank
	Fishmonger
	Environmental organisation

2

Treffpunkt **Wunschgewicht**
- gesund abnehmen
- sich ausgewogen ernähren
- schlank bleiben

über 30 leckere Diät-Mahlzeiten

4

Wintergarten-Schautag:
Sonntags 11–14 Uhr
(Keine Beratung, kein Verkauf)

alwiplast

Auf Wunsch Finanzierung

Wir fertigen auch Fenster, Türen, Rolläden u. Sonnenschutzanlagen (inkl. Montage)

Repräsentanz: Rainer Bubbel
Geöffnet: Mo.–Do. 8–17; Fr. 8–14 Uhr
● Britzer Damm 199 ●
12347 Berlin
☎ 606 60 78

1

Preisgünstige Aquarien-Sets
● Reichhaltige Auswahl ● Fachliche Beratung
Ihr Heimtier-Fachgeschäft
Zoohaus Haindl
☎ 57 11 89
Promenade
Nordwest Zentrum
FRANKFURT-NORDWESTSTADT

3

tipit
austauschbare Schmuckelemente für Ring, Kette und ...

Grundring

Ehinger-Schwarz
Schmuck-Ideen-Gestaltung

Achet Silber
Rote-Hahnen-Gasse 1a
Regensburg
Telefon (0941) 56 70 79

5

naturschutzjugend
im Naturschutzbund Deutschland (NABU) e.V.
Naturschutzjugend
Königsträßle 74
70597 Stuttgart

6

Ferienlager
und Jugendcamps
Katalog:
☎ 030-280 80 88
Falken-Jugendfahrten

7

Schenken mit Herz.

Eine Gabe von Mensch zu Mensch. Mit Geld nicht zu bezahlen. Erste Hilfe für große Not. Ihr Blut rettet Leben. Tausend Dank.

KOMM MIT! SPENDE BLUT.
BEIM ROTEN KREUZ

Weitere Informationen und Termine zur Blutspende bei Ihrem Roten Kreuz.

C

Read through the brochure information, and answer the questions <u>in English</u>.

Legoland Deutschland
Erleben, Lachen, Selbermachen
Mit vielen tollen Attraktionen und super Shows für dich und deine Familie!

Miniland

Hier findest du vieles aus Europa in Miniformat. Ganze 25 Millionen LEGO Steine wurden hier im Miniland gebraucht.
<u>Neu im Miniland:</u>
Das Schloss Neuschwanstein aus Bayern! An dem Original hat man über 20 Jahre gebaut. Wir haben es aber in nur 100 Tagen geschafft! Jetzt ist das fertige Modell mit seinen 400 Fenstern über drei Meter hoch und vier Meter lang!

1. (i) How many blocks were used in the construction of **Miniland**?

_____

(ii) *(a)* How long did it take to build the <u>model</u> of **Neuschwanstein Castle?**

_____

(b) Describe the model in detail, as per the text.

_____

_____

Lego City

Hier kannst du in der Audi LEGOLAND Fahrschule deinen ersten Führerschein machen – natürlich in Autos aus LEGO!

Kleiner Tipp: Am besten morgens gleich einen Platz in der Fahrschule reservieren.

2. **Legoland** offers a driving licence.
   (i) Where in Legoland do you get it, and what does it entitle you to drive?

   _____

   _____

   (ii) What useful tip is given?

   _____

   _____

Lego Akademie

Wenn du mit deiner Schulklasse kommst, könnt ihr hier Workshops machen. Du lernst zum Beispiel, wie du einen kleinen LEGO Roboter programmierst, damit er das macht, was du willst!

Zum LEGOLAND Park Günzburg zu kommen ist kinderleicht. Er liegt genau zwischen Stuttgart und München und ist gut mit dem Zug oder Auto zu erreichen.

3. What does the **Lego academy** offer for school groups? Give details.

   _____

   _____

   _____

4. (i) Where is **Legoland** Deutschland situated?

   _____

   _____

   (ii) How does one get to it?

   _____

D

In each of the following three questions, indicate your answer by <u>writing the</u> <u>appropriate sentence on the line provided</u>.

(i) You want permission **to sit beside your friend** for the next class. What do you ask the teacher?

(a) Darf ich hinter meinem Freund sitzen?

(b) Soll ich neben meinem Freund sitzen?

(c) Darf ich vor meinem Freund an die Tafel?

(d) Darf ich neben meinem Freund sitzen?

(ii) You are **feeling unwell in class**. What do you say?

(a) Es geht Ihnen nicht gut.

(b) Mir geht es prima.

(c) Ich fühle mich nicht wohl.

(d) Geht es euch nicht so gut?

(iii) Your teacher asks you to **hand out the copies**. What does he/she say?

(a) Teil bitte die Hefte aus.

(b) Teilt bitte die Bücher aus.

(c) Sammelt bitte die Hefte ein.

(d) Wirf das Heft bitte weg.

E

Read through the following notices advertising **extra-curricular activities** in your German exchange school. Then fill in the information required, **in English**, in the spaces provided. The required information from box (1) has been filled in as an example.

(1) Literaturgruppe
Luise Dietrich, Deutschlehrerin, bietet einen Literaturklub für Schüler aus den Klassen 11–13 an. Man liest Gedichte und schreibt auch Kurzgeschichten und Aufsätze. Wann: Jeden Dienstagabend von sieben bis halb neun. Wo: In der Schulbibliothek.

(2) Karate für Mädchen
Immer mehr Mädchen fühlen sich nicht mehr sicher auf dem Heimweg von der Schule. Jetzt will Herr Müller von der Karateschule Dresden helfen. Er bietet eine Mischung aus Karate und Judo für alle Altersgruppen an. Der Kurs dauert 12 Wochen und findet montags von 14.00–16.00 Uhr in der Turnhalle statt. Kosten: €24.

(3) Schachklub
Für Schüler der Klassen 5 und 6 bietet Theo Balder aus der Klasse 13 auch dieses Jahr wieder einen Schachklub an. Interesse?
Komm doch am Donnerstag um 13.30 Uhr zum Erdkunderaum!
Eine Stunde lang zeigt Theo, wie man Schach spielt und wie man besser wird. Er organisiert auch Spiele gegen andere Schulen.

(4) Chemieklub
Können wir Gold aus Metall machen? Unser Chemielehrer Herr Vogel will es mit einem Trick versuchen. Wer will bei interessanten Experimenten mitmachen? Jeden Samstagmorgen von 9.00 bis 11.00 Uhr trifft sich Herr Vogel mit seinen Helfern im Labor. Alle Schüler der Goethe-Schule sind wilkommen.
Tipps und Tricks in Chemie – Naturwissenschaften machen Spaß!

	Activity	For whom	Content	When	Where
(1)	Literature group	11th, 12th and 13th class.	Read poetry, write short stories and essays.	Tuesday, 7–8.30pm.	School library.
(2)					
(3)					
(4)					

Read through this article and answer the questions below <u>in English</u>.

Ran an den Ball

"Ich will nur noch Hockey spielen"
Seit sechs Jahren gibt es für die 14-jährige Annika Neuhaus aus Essen nichts anderes mehr als Hockey spielen. Im Sommer draußen auf dem Spielfeld, im Herbst und Winter drinnen in der Turnhalle – Hockey hat immer Saison! Das ganze Jahr hindurch trainiert Annika zweimal in der Woche im Essener Hockey-Club, HCE 1899.

"Ich liebe es, schnell zu rennen"
Beim Hallenhockey müssen die Spieler sogar noch viel schneller sein als beim Hockey draußen im Sommer, denn das Spielfeld in der Halle ist viel kleiner als das Feld draußen. "In der Halle muss man echt schnell sein", erklärt Annika uns, "der Ball ist einfach immer im Spiel, weil es keine Seitenlinie gibt! Wenn wir draußen Hockey spielen, hat das Spielfeld immer eine Seitenlinie. Da darf der Ball nicht drüber gehen."

"Meinen Hockeyschläger hab' ich mir jetzt selbst gekauft"
Mit acht Jahren bekam Annika ihren ersten Schläger vom Club. "Jetzt ist alles anders. Ich habe mir meinen neuen Schläger für 40€ selbst gekauft. Ich trage beim Spielen einen grünen Rock, ein T-Shirt und spezielle grüne Strümpfe, Turnschuhe für die Halle und Turnschuhe für draußen. Es ist ein absolutes Muss, meine Zähne und Beine zu schützen, besonders beim Hallenhockey."

"Im Mittelfeld spiel' ich am liebsten"
Annikas Lieblingspositionen sind vorne rechts und im Mittelfeld. "Vorne rechts ist man immer sehr aktiv. Das mag ich. Und vom Mittelfeld kann man die meisten Tore schießen", meint Annika. Das tut sie besonders gern und gut. In einem Spiel hat sie sogar schon vier Tore geschossen. "Wenn ich mal keine Tore schieße, ist das auch nicht so schlimm", lacht Annika.

"Das große Hockey-Turnier im Mai finde ich supercool"
Jeden Mai fährt Annika mit ihrer Hockey-Mannschaft zu einem richtig großen Turnier. Dann spielen sie vier Tage lang nur Hockey. "Wir wohnen dann alle auf einem Campingplatz. Es ist supercool, so viele andere Teams aus Deutschland, der Schweiz und Belgien zu treffen und gegeneinander zu spielen. Wir haben immer so viel Spaß!"

1. *(a)* For which club does Annika play hockey?   *(b)* How often does she train?
(Paragraph 1)

(a) _____

(b) _____

2. How does **indoor** hockey differ from **outdoor** hockey, according to the article? Give details.   **(Paragraph 2)**

_____

_____

_____

_____

3. What equipment and gear does Annika need for hockey? Give details.
(Paragraph 3)

_____

_____

_____

_____

4. What are Annika's favourite playing positions, and why?   **(Paragraph 4)**

_____

_____

_____

5. Annika takes part in a hockey tournament every year.
   (a) What details are mentioned about it?
   (b) Which countries participate in the tournament?   **(Paragraph 5)**

(a) _____

_____

_____

(b) _____

_____

G

Answer <u>in English</u> the questions which follow the passage.

Der Unfall

Es ist mittags um halb eins. Der Schulunterricht ist
gerade zu Ende und alle Schüler gehen nach Hause.
Vor der Schule geht es chaotisch zu. Die Kleinen
rennen hinaus, während die größeren Schüler noch
herumstehen und miteinander sprechen. Sie holen   5
ihre Fahrräder und Mopeds, und einige Abiturienten
haben sogar schon Autos.

Der fünfzehnjährige Paul steht unten an der
Schultreppe und wartet auf Alexa. Paul hat sein Fahrrad
und auch das Fahrrad von Alexa schon aus dem Fahrradkeller der Schule geholt. Alexa ist eine 10
Klasse unter ihm. Die beiden fahren immer zusammen nach Hause, weil sie fast denselben Weg
haben. Paul mag Alexa, besonders ihre schönen schwarzen Haare und ihre dunkelbraunen
Augen. Alexa geht gern in die Schule. Sie erzählt Paul immer sofort, was am Tag in der Klasse
passiert ist. Ob sie gute oder schlechte Noten bekommen hat. Ob die Lehrer geschimpft haben.
Ob der Unterricht Spaß gemacht hat. Wer etwas Lustiges gesagt hat.   15

Jetzt kommt Alexa endlich die Treppe hinunter. Sie lacht und zeigt Paul ein Bild, das sie in
Kunst gemalt hat. In diesem Moment hören Paul und Alexa die Bremsen eines Autos kreischen.
Sie drehen sofort die Köpfe und sehen auf die Straße. Ein Junge fliegt durch die Luft, landet auf
einem Auto, fällt auf die Straße und bleibt ganz still liegen.

„Udo", flüstert Alexa schockiert. Udo? Jetzt erkennt auch Paul den Jungen auf der Straße. Es ist 20
der jüngere Bruder seines besten Freundes. Paul läuft auf die Straße und geht zu ihm. Es ist
wirklich Udo. Udo öffnet die Augen und scheint nicht zu wissen, wo er ist. „Udo? Wie geht es
dir? Wo tut es dir weh? Kannst du mich verstehen?", fragt Paul.

„Paul", sagt Udo leise. „Ich habe das Auto nicht gesehen. Es kam ja so schnell um die Ecke!"
Jetzt ist Alexa auch da. „Wir müssen die Polizei und einen Krankenwagen rufen", sagt Alexa. 25
„Hol auch seinen Bruder vom Sportplatz. Und den Klassenlehrer von Udo!", fügt Paul hinzu.
„Keine Polizei", sagt Udo, „so schlimm ist es alles nicht."

---

1. What happens when school is over? Give details. **(Lines 1–7)**

_____

_____

_____

_____

2. *(a)* What information is given about Alexa? Give details. **(Lines 10–13)**
  (b) Alexa always tells Paul what happened in class. Give examples of what
      she tells him. **(Lines 13–15)**

  (a) _____

  _____

  _____

  (b) _____

  _____

  _____

3. Describe the accident that Paul and Alexa witness. **(Lines 17–19)**

_____

_____

_____

4. *(a)* Who is the injured boy? Give details. **(Lines 20–22)**
  (b) What questions does Paul ask the injured boy? **(Lines 22–23)**

  (a) _____

  _____

  (b) _____

  _____

5. Whom does *(a)* Alexa and *(b)* Paul want to contact straight away?
      (Lines 25–26)

  (a) Alexa _____

  (b) Paul _____

Section III – Written Expression
(80 marks)

The **lined pages** which follow the questions are to be used for answering (**A**) and (**B**).

A
LETTER
You have recently received a letter from your German exchange partner. Write a letter in reply, answering all the questions (which have been numbered for you) in some detail. **(120 words minimum)**

Cuxhaven, den 26. Mai 2004

Liebe/r ....,
ich finde es klasse, dass du mit deinen Eltern im Sommer nach Deutschland kommst. Ich freue mich schon total darauf, dich zu sehen. (**1**) Wann kommt ihr denn genau? Kommt ihr mit der Fähre oder dem Flugzeug? Wie lange dauert die Reise eigentlich?

Du weißt sicher schon, wo ihr übernachtet. (**2**) Habt ihr schon ein Hotel oder eine andere Unterkunft gebucht? Bei uns ist auch Platz zum Übernachten, wenn ihr wollt. Was meinst du? (**3**) Wollt ihr ein Auto mieten oder bringt ihr das eigene Auto?

Wenn meine Eltern und ich Urlaub machen, machen wir immer Aktivurlaub. (**4**) Wie ist es denn in deiner Familie? Was wollt ihr hier in Deutschland alles machen?

Ich habe letzte Woche mein Zeugnis bekommen. Die Noten waren nicht besonders gut und meine Eltern waren richtig sauer! (**5**) Was für Noten bekommst du normalerweise in der Schule? Was ist dein Lieblingsfach, und warum? Welches Fach machst du nicht so gern? Warum nicht?

Du warst doch letzte Woche beim Robbie Williams Konzert, oder? (**6**) Wo war das nochmal? Wie bist du dort hingekommmen? Wie hast du das Konzert gefunden? Ich finde die Musik von Robbie super!

Das wär's für heute.
Viel Spaß beim Urlaub planen!

Dein(e)
Michi

_____
_____
_____
_____
_____
_____
_____
_____
_____
_____
_____
_____
_____

B

POSTCARD

You are with your family on holiday and write a postcard to your **German** penpal. Include the following details:

- Say where you are and how long you are staying
- Describe the bad weather
- Say how you find the food
- Mention two things you did yesterday.

(Write approximately **25–30** words)

_____
_____
_____
_____
_____